Th
Memoirs
of an
Artillery
Forward Observer
1944-1945

MW00805777

The
Memoirs
of an
Artillery
Forward Observer
1944-1945

by
James Russell Major

Sunflower University Press®

1531 Yuma • P. O. Box 1009 • Manhattan, Kansas 66505-1009 USA

© 1999 J. Russell Major

Printed in the United States of America on acid-free paper.

Edited by Sonie Liebler

Layout by Lori L. Daniel

ISBN 0-89745-229-1

Sunflower University Press is a wholly-owned subsidiary
of the non-profit 501(c)3 Journal of the West, Inc.

To
Burton D. Isenhour, who was with me from the beginning to the end
Colen M. Hoyle, Missing In Action December 6, 1944
Ray Speaker, Mortally Wounded December 26, 1944
and
Raymond H. Bradshaw, John W. Currie, and William J. Jedrzejek,
who also served so ably and bravely on my forward observer team.

Contents

James Russell Major, 1943.

Foreword

$\mathcal{T}$HE NOTED HISTORIAN OF European affairs at Emory University, James Russell Major, was one of the key, yet unsung, officers of the U.S. Army after D-Day in Europe in 1944-1945.

As an Artillery Forward Observer, his job was to move up with the infantry, of which he and his team were a vital part, and to direct fire onto the enemy in support of the infantry from batteries in the rear of the fighting front.

This is the rare story of a very small unit and its immense contribution to victory. It is a human story of a young man growing up, and becoming immensely proud of his skill at directing U.S. Army guns onto targets of opportunity in fluid action and unpredictable mobile warfare.

Robin Higham
Professor of History *Emeritus*
Kansas State University

Introduction

FTER I COMPLETED MY LAST PROJECT IN European history, I turned to writing an account of my family's long sojourn in Virginia. When I came to the American Civil War of 1861-1865, I discovered that almost nothing was known of the adventures and reflections of my grandfather and his three brothers. The oldest was killed in the Battle of Seven Pines in 1862 while he was still in his teens. The youngest was one of John S. Mosby's men. My grandfather and his brother, Will, were artillery privates. In the Battle of the Crater Sam, during the siege of Petersburg in 1864, my grandfather is reputed to have crawled forward and directed fire into the vast hole by signaling with his arms. I am, therefore, not the first member of my family to be an artillery forward observer.

To prevent my activities and thoughts from being lost as my grandfather's have been, I have decided to write the following account for the benefit of my posterity. A second and equally important motive is to record the actions of the men who accompanied me.

I totally lost track of them when I left my battalion just after World War II, and have never properly thanked them for all they did.

The events I now record took place over a half-century ago, but happily there are some documents to assist my memory. A brief history of the 90th Infantry Division was published just after the war, and at my father's request I wrote in the margins what I was doing when this or that was taking place. In 1950, H. M. Cole's massive *The Lorraine Campaign* appeared, and I once more recorded my role in the margins. At that time, I could still remember the infantry units I was with and often the names of the officers.

My mother saved my Randolph-Macon Academy and Virginia Military Institute report cards and the weekly letters I wrote home while I was at V.M.I. and in the Army. Unfortunately I strictly observed the censorship rules. As a result, my letters lacked military details and the desired precision as to time and place. When I think of the diaries and revealing letters I now know many generals wrote at the time, it makes me angry. In my position, I knew nothing that would do the Germans any good, but the high-ranking officers' comments certainly might have been of use if they had fallen into enemy hands.

I have most of my military orders and have obtained a few additional records from the National Personnel Records Center in St. Louis, Missouri. Of greater value were the surviving official records of the 949th Field Artillery Battalion in the National Archives at College Park, Maryland, in which are included a brief history of the battalion, all the After Action Reports, and occasionally other documents such as the number and kinds of rounds fired at this or that time, logs of messages received, etc. It is amazing the amount of paperwork that was supposed to be kept. One wonders how there was time to win the war. The answer, I suspect, is that the responsible officers often went three or four days without writing anything, and then, when they had some spare time, recorded events to the best of their memory.

In a few instances I know that the official records are wrong, and I am suspicious of some others. But as a rule I have accepted the records, except when I am certain they are incorrect.

Eugene M. White, Jr., kindly gave me a roster that contains the given names of those who served in B Battery, 949th Field Artillery Battalion, for the period he was its commander. We called each other by our surnames, and often did not know the given names of those we worked with in the most intimate, life-threatening situations for many months. I am also indebted to him and to Lee G. Cass, Donald W. Kilbourn, and Edward C. Seddon for clarifying some issues and for most of the photographs. Blair, my wife, and Blair Louise Flaschka, my eldest daughter, read and criticized the manuscript. The former also prepared the map of the Battle of the Bulge. Without the assistance of all of the above, these memoirs would have suffered.

A few events I still remember as clearly as the day they happened. Many others that are mentioned in the official military records, I have totally forgotten. My account is as accurate as I could make it and is much more precise for the war in 1944 than for 1945, because of my notes I had made in the book on the 90th Division and the study by H. M. Cole. I have not used footnotes, except in the introduction, because if anyone is interested, he can easily find the source from the text.

There are those who will accuse me of bias. I can only say that most of the opinions I offer are well-grounded in fact. I regard General George S. Patton as being by far the best American general in the war — one of the few things that Hitler and his generals did agree on. Our Army was largely mechanized. In spite of the famed panzer tank divisions, only a small part of the German army moved by motor.

Time and again when General Patton broke through the German lines, he sought permission to make a wide envelopment and capture the German army, only to be restrained. The risk was slight even if his troops had been momentarily cut off.

We had complete control of the air and greatly outnumbered the Germans. The fact that Patton alone, of the Army commanders, understood how to use a mobile army is gradually becoming recognized. As Martin Blumenson, a leading authority, has recently noted:

> It took some years after the war for the fullness of Patton's stature to emerge. Unlike most of his contemporaries, whose reputations have steadily declined since the war, Patton's has continued to rise. This phenomenon has occurred despite the relatively low role he held in the chain of command.[1]

I never saw General Patton, and as far as I know nobody in our battalion had more than a glimpse of him before the end of the war; yet we were always conscious of his leadership. We were all well aware that we were in the Third Army and were proud of it. There were jokes about "our blood and his guts," a play on the General's nickname, but this did not detract from his image as a great leader.

How Patton managed to impose his personality on an entire army is a mystery. Few officers are able to inspire a battalion or even a battery to the degree he did over several hundred thousand men.

He was emotionally unstable, and there were serious blemishes on his character. I do not refer to the soldier-slapping incidents. I was once tempted to punch a cowardly private into doing his duty, and at times I still wish I had. The tragedy of those events was that they caused General Omar N. Bradley, not Patton, to command the American Army group in France. Had Patton enjoyed equal status with Field Marshal Bernard L. Montgomery, he might have been able to impose his strategy on General Dwight D. Eisenhower and ended the war in 1944. Thousand of lives would have been saved.

In part, Patton's very eccentricities contributed to his image. He visited our battalion's Observation Post on August 14, 1945, when a training mission was being fired. He witnessed a superb adjustment and fire for effect by B Battery. Overcome, he told our forward observer, "It would be a pleasure to be killed by fire like that."[2] What other general would have made such a statement? It reflected his strange character, and also what a fine battalion we had. I only wish that I had been conducting the fire, but by then I had been in the States for over two months.

A second area where I might be accused of bias is my admiration of the infantry and my belief that the air force was pampered and overrated. An airman is in danger only when he is engaged in battle. When his mission is over, he returns to his base where he can take a shower, enjoy an adequate meal, sleep in a warm bed, and feel secure until his next assignment. He gets a medal for every few missions, and after he has received enough of them, he is rotated home. The damage he inflicted on the enemy has been greatly overrated. From my experience, it often seemed to me that our airmen were as likely to attack us as the enemy. I have been strafed by

American and German planes a half-dozen times, but only once was anyone hit. The only time I was ever near an exploding bomb, it had been
dropped by one of our planes. Doubtless, it was intended to land on the
Germans on the other side of a flooded river that was at least a half-mile
wide.

The life of an infantryman is quite different. He may go for weeks,
indeed months, without a shower. He sweats in his wool uniform in the
summer and freezes in it in the winter. He lives in the dirt. His home is
the foxhole or, at best, a smoke-filled house that is so packed with his
comrades that he is lucky to have the space to stretch out. For days at a
time he lives on K rations and, occasionally, even this meager diet is not
available. He is in the greatest danger in an attack, but he is never truly
safe. At any moment a shell may crash at his side, a sniper may take a shot
at him, or he may step on a mine that blows his legs off. It is easy to be
brave when one is comfortable, but the misery and constant danger of an
infantryman's life gradually make him fatalistic. He begins to say, "When
I get it." To him it is only a question of whether he will be killed, be per-
manently disabled, or get the "million-dollar" wound that would put him
in the hospital for a few months' rest but cause no permanent damage. The
greatest injustice of the war was that the airman received extra pay for his
occasionally dangerous but comfortable life while the infantryman was an
unsung and under-recompensed hero.

The Germans held the American infantrymen in low repute. Certainly
they fell below German standards, but, with rare exceptions, they did their
duty in spite of their miserable way of life. War correspondent Ernie Pyle
spent time with nearly every branch of the service, but the infantry was his
favorite. They were the "brave men" par excellence. I wholeheartedly con-
cur with his judgment.

The artillery finally came into its own in World War II. "The same Germans who disparaged American infantry consistently praised American
artillery."[3] "The Second World War was an artillery war; over half the
battle casualties were caused by artillery fire, in spite of the commonly
held view that tanks and air power were the dominant weapons."[4] Artillery
was justly called, by Boyd L. Dastrup, the *King of Battle.*[5]

I confess that I was surprised to learn what an important role the artillery had played when I began to write this book. It was only a combination of forces that made it possible for the cannon to become the preeminent weapon. During the Civil War, artillery was far less important than the infantry and the cavalry. Artillery relied almost entirely on direct fire. The gunner aimed at a target that was likely to be less than a thousand yards away. Often he was within small-arms range of the enemy. In the rare instances when the target was not visible, someone had to crawl forward and adjust fire by signaling with his arms or with flags.

By World War I, the telephone had become effective. It was the great age of the Observation Post. An officer would set up his OP on a hill, in a building, or wherever he could get a view of the target area. Aided by a bc (battery commander)-telescope that measured horizontal and vertical angles, a range finder, and other complex equipment, he telephoned his commands to his battery that might be several miles away. The trouble was he had no direct contact with the attacking infantry. The infantry thus lost the close artillery support it had enjoyed during the Civil War.

By World War II, the radio was available and had come into its own. Small two-passenger liaison planes could now assist the crews that manned the Observation Posts. Forward observers could accompany the infantry and with their radios provide the direct support that had been absent in 1918, during World War I. The development of fire-direction centers enabled us to mass the fire of one or more battalions on a given target, ammunition was improved, and in the course of World War II a fuse came into use that would explode a shell at the desired height over the target and penetrate the deepest foxholes.

Yet in spite of the great role played by the artillery, pride of place must still go to the infantry. The artillerymen who remained with the batteries were always within artillery range of the enemy, but they usually escaped small-arms fire. In the winter they had large tents and a stove that provided surprising warmth. Except during periods of rapid movement, they had enough to eat. They literally went months without a shower, but they could use their helmets for sponge baths. Their lot was far less deluxe than the airman, but they were better off than the infantry. Only those who accompanied the infantry as forward observers fully shared the doughboys' dangers and hardships.

A third bias I might be accused of is a dislike of the high brass and the rear-echelon troops. Once I was sent back to 20th Corps headquarters on an errand and found some officers spending more time chasing the Red Cross girls than fighting the war. There was even a sign that read "general officers latrine." Thus, the generals were separated from the colonels and, of course, the officers from the enlisted men. I can readily understand the desire for privacy, but all those in the front lines were equals.

Corps, division, and even battalion staffs need at least a tent and tables to spread their maps on and do their work, but they didn't need chateaux. There were far too many rear-echelon support troops and, often, they got equipment that should have gone to the front-line soldiers. I saw soldiers in Reims with rubbers to keep their shoes dry as they walked on paved streets, but few infantrymen had more than their leather boots to separate their feet from mud and snow. No wonder we sometimes lost more men from trench foot and frostbite than to enemy fire.

During the war I almost never saw an officer with a rank higher than captain who was in danger from small-arms fire. In the Civil War, generals led their men in battle. I suspect that their casualty rate was higher than the privates. In the war in Europe, senior officers in infantry divisions were rarely in serious danger or long uncomfortable. Outside of Paris I saw only two generals. General James A. Van Fleet, who then commanded the 90th Infantry Division, was in a jeep and had stopped at a crossroads. The other was in the rear, awarding decorations. A senior officer loses control of his men if he is too close to the front, but as far as is practical he ought to share their dangers and hardships.

What was most disgraceful was the way they passed out medals to each other for gallantry. Patton's deputy chief of staff was awarded the Distinguished Service Cross for making a personal reconnaissance of the 90th Division bridgehead over the Moselle River. Thousands of men who had taken and held the bridgehead received nothing.[6] There are medals for efficiency that would have been more appropriate.

A final charge that may be made is that I show too much respect for the Germans. I was struck from the time we arrived in France by frequent French comments on how free we were to forage for supplements to our diet. Germans, I gather, were strictly forbidden to trespass on civilian property. As early as September 24, 1944, I wrote my mother: "The more I see the Germans the more I admire them. They are wonderful soldiers and have put up an unbelievably clean fight." The death camps were then unknown. Along with the horrors they were to reveal, we should consider the German humanitarian acts.

When the 83rd Infantry Division suffered heavy casualties in Normandy, the opposing German commander returned the medics his troops had captured. In the accompanying note he said that he thought they were needed, and he expressed the hope that if the situation were ever reversed, the Americans would return the favor.[7] This was not a lone incident, and such actions should be weighed against the unbelievable acts of cruelty perpetrated by the Nazis, a group of thugs who achieved positions of power. It is a tragedy that they disgraced one of the finest armies Europe has ever seen, one that on the western front obeyed the laws of war as well as we did.

Every story should have a theme. It is a necessary literary device to give shape, form, and direction. If I were using the data I have collected to write an account of another man, my theme would probably be the story of how a bookish recluse who knew nothing of firearms and was woefully lacking self-confidence was slowly transformed into a decorated officer with the highest possible combat efficiency rating. As a literary device it might work, but it would not be strictly true. I never had a clear idea in what direction I was headed, and much that happened to me was dictated by chance.

However, I do believe that the driving force of my life was a sense of duty instilled in me by my parents, reinforced by the books I read as a child, and nurtured at V.M.I. At school I tried to make good grades because it was my duty to do so. When at college, I wrote home once a week and did my best to adhere to that schedule when I was in combat, to relieve my parents' anxiety. The problem was that my sense of obligation was very limited. I knew that I was no athlete when I went to V.M.I., and I soon found out that I was no soldier. I had no interest in extra-curricular activities such as serving on one of the cadet publications. V.M.I. made a conscientious effort to educate the whole man, but I did not feel that it was my duty to try to be a good athlete, soldier, or active participant in school affairs. I ceased to try after my freshman "rat" year. Here, a second motivating force became a factor — pride in the sense that I did not like to fail. I avoided activities where I had little opportunity of success. It was only when in combat that I expanded my conception of duty to include the soldier. I had found a job that suited me and felt duty-bound to do all I could to help the infantry. But these observations are all hindsight.

I leave it to you, "gentle reader," as writers used to say, to explain why things happened as they did. I can only say that I have reported the war as I saw it. I have included events and rumors that have been left out of the official records and have told my own story as honestly as I could.

My mistakes and disappointments are included along with my few triumphs.

NOTES

1. Martin Blumenson, *The Battle of the Generals* (New York: Morrow, 1993), 271. For Hitler's opinion of Patton see David Irving, *Hitler's War* (New York: Macmillan, 1977), 683-684. For the German general's opinion see Martin Blumenson, *Patton* (New York: Macmillan, 1985), 296.
2. "949 Field Artillery Battalion Unit History," 5. National Archives at College Park, Maryland. Information from Lieutenant Lee Cass.
3. Norman Polmar and Thomas B. Allen, eds., *World War II: America at War 1941-1945* (New York: Random House, 1991), 106.
4. I. C. B. Dear, ed., *The Oxford Companion to World War II* (Oxford: Oxford University Press, 1995), 57. From 25 to 30 percent of the Third Army soldiers admitted to the hospital in August-December 1944 were wounded by gunshots, and from 50 to 60 percent by explosives. As the German infantry was superior to ours and as we had many times more cannon and much more ammunition than they had, it is probable that at least two-thirds of the casualties we inflicted were done by the artillery. Hugh M. Cole, *The Ardennes: Battle of the Bulge* (Washington, D.C.: Office of the Chief of Military History, Department of the Army, 1965), 656.
5. Boyd L. Dastrup, *King of Battle* (Fort Monroe, VA: Office of the Command Historian, U.S. Army Training and Doctrine Command, 1992).
6. Hugh M. Cole, *The Lorraine Campaign* (Washington, D.C.: Historical Division, Department of the Army, 1950), 396n.
7. Martin Blumenson, *Breakout and Pursuit* (Washington, D.C.: Center of Military History, U.S. Army, 1984), 83-84.

Chapter 1

Childhood

I WAS BORN ON January 7, 1921, in the front room of Riverside, the family home in Riverton, Virginia. The unincorporated village was located at the junction of the north and south forks of the Shenandoah River in northern Virginia. The census taken a few months before my birth recorded 404 inhabitants; my arrival swelled the population to 405, unless someone else had come or departed in the meantime.

Riverside was a large brick house situated on a hill overlooking the south fork of the river and with a beautiful view across the fields to the Massanutten Mountains. At that time the house had been in my mother's family for only seven decades. It had just been remodeled in time for my arrival. The kitchen, which was connected with the house only by a covered causeway, had been torn down and a new one added on the north side of the house. A porch had been built on the south side, but most important, central heating, plumbing, and electricity had been installed. By contemporary standards the house was still rather primitive. The coal furnace provided adequate heat for the central rooms but not the wings. There was only one upstairs bathroom to serve six bedrooms, and the half-bath off the pantry was more for servants than members of the family. Nevertheless, my parents looked on Riverside as a modern home. For them it was. They had been accustomed to fireplaces, outhouses, and well water.

When I was a child, there were still signs of the former plantation house. The slave quarters and smokehouse had been torn down, but for many years it had been difficult to get grass to grow where the latter had stood because of the salt embedded in the soil. The barn had been retained to provide a home for a cow and a roof for two automobiles.

In the south side of the front yard there was a sunken area where ice had been buried. In the old days it had been customary to cut ice off the river during the winter and preserve it deep in the ground for summer use. By 1920, ice was manufactured, and in my childhood it was delivered daily in a truck. Occasionally, we bought a few extra pounds, packed it with salt around the ice cream freezer, filled the container with real cream from the cow, and with much labor cranked it until it became frozen. I don't remember my mother ever buying ice cream before the war.

Riverside was a big house. The ceilings were high, and with several exceptions the rooms were large. Two parlors, two halls, a library, and a dining room provided an unusual amount of space for entertainment, but the upstairs was crowded.

My father's brother Fayette lived with us. Fayette had contracted cerebrospinal meningitis when he was five, and his brain had ceased to develop. He stoked the furnace, worked in the half-acre garden, and tended the cow that acted as the lawn mower.

My mother also had a relative by marriage who lived at Riverside. Her Uncle Henry had died leaving his wife very little, and her only son passed away during the great influenza epidemic. With Aunt Gussie in one bedroom and Fayette in another, there were only four for the remainder of the family. The front room was reserved for guests, reducing the total to three, hardly enough when two sisters followed me, bringing the number of children to five. Furthermore, a bedroom had to be crossed to reach the one on either wing. The result was that we were packed together as closely as in any colonial or antebellum family. At the age of 77, I still have never had a room to myself.

Two miles away, the county seat, Front Royal, was a sleepy place until the American Viscose Corporation built a plant there shortly before the war. Culpeper, a town southeast of us, had a traffic light, but our county seat had none, a fact that sorely troubled me in my childhood. One would think that a boy raised in such rural surroundings would become the master of country lore — of horseback riding, hunting, fishing, and the like. Such was not the case. Riverside stood on a two- or three-acre lot, not a farm. We had no horses, and I don't remember ever trying to mount one before I went to Virginia Military Institute. My father had a 12-gauge shotgun, which he occasionally used to shoot starlings from the south porch. I fired it once or twice, and for a brief period I had a .22-caliber rifle, which I used to shoot bottles off the fence, but I have never been hunting in my life. Several times I attempted to fish in the Shenandoah River, but even then there was little to catch except sun perch. Lazy though I was, fishing was too inactive and boring to have any attraction.

I need not have been so isolated. My older brother and sister had many friends who were happy to walk two miles from Front Royal to play tennis on our court. There were no swimming pools in the county, but there was a beach on the river several hundred yards south of the house. Swimming there was far more interesting than in a pool. The river was bigger, and it was always exciting to explore its bottom. An island with a sandbar divided it in half, and a worn-down dam provided a rapid current in some places and eddies in others to carry the swimmer back upstream. In spite of our relative isolation, my brother and sisters developed sufficient social graces and charm to draw friends to their side, but for some reason it led me to withdraw within myself. I never acquired the self-confidence or social poise that was typical of well-balanced children.

My most frequent companion was Sonny Smith. The Smiths lived on the hill on the other side of the river. Our mothers were close friends, and Sonny's father had graduated from V.M.I. four years after mine. Our parents' ties and our close proximity threw us together, although it was hard to imagine two more different boys. He was chunky; I was lean. My mother sometimes called us Laurel and Hardy. More important, he hated anything that smelled of the academic. He almost never read a book, and loved to hang around the filling station, just below his house. I loved books and hated anything mechanical. I never learned to drive a nail straight. We nevertheless shared many childhood adventures.

The county had only one high school. The first eight grades for the children of Front Royal, Riverton, and nearby villages were taught in the same building. Only the more distant villages had their own grade schools. When I was only five, I began the first grade in a private school taught by Miss Mary and Miss Nettie Weaver. There had been only one other pupil in Miss Nettie's third-grade class. After some criticism of my handwriting and English, she had become reconciled to my work and had given me straight As on the last two of the six-week reports and my exams. As the school had no fourth grade, I then transferred to the high school, where I was assigned to Miss Hoskins' room. The change was quite a shock. Now I was in a room with 30 or 40 somewhat older children I did not know, and I was subject to a strict disciplinarian and a tough grader. My grades tumbled, and my handwriting was subject to harsh but well-deserved criticism. Academically it was not a good year, but I did become adjusted to my fellow students.

On the exterior of either side of the building there were metal staircases that served as fire escapes. I soon became aware of the game of putting several boys under the staircase who were supposed to try to fight their way out. I became a favorite prisoner because I struggled so hard to escape. Needless to say, this practice led to many fights. By the end of the school year, I was accepted.

The following fall when my friend Sonny and I were wrestling in the schoolyard, a group of boys surrounded us yelling, cheering, pushing, and shoving. Until then I had always been able to beat him, because I was a year older and his extra pounds were more blubber than muscle. Somehow, he was pushed on top of me, and his weight was so great that I was unable to throw him off. At this point Miss Hoskins appeared, broke up the fight, and sent Sonny and me to our respective rooms. An hour or two later we received a summons to the principal's office.

Mr. Gasque was a far abler man than a little school like ours deserved. Short, powerfully built, his very presence commanded obedience. When we entered his office, he was working on some papers. He left us standing uncomfortably for at least 15 minutes. When he finally spoke, Sonny insisted that we had not been fighting and that other boys had caused the problem by pushing us around. Sonny's account was true enough from his point of view, but when I found that I was losing, it had become a fight for me. I let him do the talking, and we were soon allowed to leave. The episode was a turning point in my life. From that time on, I avoided fights and rarely mixed with other boys at school. I don't know why the episode affected me so. The worst Mr. Gasque would have done was to tell my father. And I suspect my father would have been pleased, provided it did not happen too often. Nevertheless, from that time I became more and more a recluse.

That same fall, my ninth year, I was taken to the hospital in Winchester to have my tonsils removed. I had a hemorrhage that the doctor was able to stop only after I had lost a large quantity of blood. Blood transfusions were far from common, and I was weak and sickly for many months, until my strength was restored.

But neither the Gasque episode nor the surgery made me a total recluse. We had a canoe, and Sonny and I used it to explore parts of the river that could only be reached by boat. Once we camped with two other boys by a cliff across the river, facing where the country club now stands. Most often we stayed at our family cabin in the Fort Valley. A creek flowed through the property, and there was a swimming hole that could not be seen from the road. We hiked all over the surrounding mountains. One dark night we threw firecrackers into a campsite about a mile from our cabin. An irate camper came out of his tent and fired a few rounds in our direction. He aimed low, not in the air, and several bullets missed us by only a few yards. We fled, leaving the camper in possession of the field. It was my first time under fire, and I earnestly hoped it would be my last.

One Halloween, Sonny and I set off on foot for Front Royal after dark to have some fun. The custom of accepting a treat in return for not doing a trick had not reached our part of the world. I suspect that we would have scorned the idea even if it had. After pouring molasses on Mr. Gasque's porch, we began to throw rocks at a street light. Happily, we were such poor baseball players that we never scored a hit. Eventually, we came to a row of parked cars in front of a house where our parents were guests at a large bridge party. We immediately set to work letting air out of the tires.

Being genuinely fond of our parents, we spared theirs. I suspect that they would have preferred us to have been less devoted when they emerged from the party with the other guests and found their cars alone unharmed. No Sherlock Holmes was needed to uncover the culprits.

The initiative for our various adventures always lay with Sonny. If left alone, I would have spent my time reading books in the library. I don't remember when the love of books began, but I had certainly been entrapped by the time I had had my tonsils out. My mother had stayed at the hospital with me and read one G. A. Henty novel after another. I have never known anyone who could read so well. Usually she was too occupied to be indulgent, but when a child became sick, she dropped everything else. I kept her busy while recovering from the operation, and then struck out on my own with the Henty books being my first favorites.

Henty was a British imperialist, and his favorite topic was the triumphs of the empire. He also occasionally tackled other subjects such as the Dutch revolt against Spain, the American Civil War, and even ancient Egypt. Whatever the setting, the story was always the same. There was a brave and responsible teenage boy who met every danger with courage and success, and a girl who occasionally had to be rescued. There was no romance, but at the end Henty might say that they were eventually married, and, if English, our hero would be elected to Parliament.

From Henty I progressed to Edgar Rice Burroughs and his stories of Tarzan and Mars. Then came such romances as Paul Leicester Ford's *Janice Merdith*, and Stanley Weyman's *A Gentleman of France*. Once more the hero was always courageous and the heroine virtuous. She was permitted to have pride, and her pride and misunderstandings provided the suspense in the romantic aspects of the books. In our well-stocked library there were multi-volume sets of James Fenimore Cooper, Charles Dickens, and Sir Walter Scott, and also of Alexandre Dumas, Honoré de Balzac, Guy de Maupassant, and Théophile Gautier in translation. My mother's favorite was Dickens.

Another influence in my childhood was Miss Virginia Dorsey, Ginny, as we called her, an elderly lady who lived in genteel poverty with her widowed sister. Their father had been a doctor noted for his hospitality and his devotion to the Southern cause; so devoted, indeed, that he had little to leave his daughters. Ginny looked after us on occasions, and my mother discreetly rewarded her in a way not to give offense. There were no school buses in the early days. We were taken to school and back and forth to lunch by my father, whose preserving plant was nearby. After school, we went to Ginny's several blocks away to wait for my mother to pick us up.

Ginny was supposed to have been in love with my grandfather. Perhaps it was for this reason she took an interest in me, his namesake. In any case, she was determined that I should have a proper Southern upbringing. When I was in her charge, she read to me from her favorite author, Sir Walter Scott. She also told me stories of the horrors the Yankees had perpetrated. Once when I referred to my father as daddy, she told me I mustn't call him that. Daddy was a Yankee word.

Ginny's proudest moment had been when she was crowned queen of a tournament in 1870. When she died, she left me a large portrait of Robert E. Lee, which now hangs in my study. Her furniture went to my mother. In one piece, we found several thousand dollars in Confederate bonds and money. So passed one of the last of the true Southern ladies of whom I have fond memories.

It was hardly necessary for Ginny to feed me Southern lore. It was deeply impregnated in Riverside. Bullets had chipped its brick walls, and General Thomas "Stonewall" Jackson had spent the night there after winning the battle of Front Royal in 1862. A small table was placed on the front porch where he could receive couriers from the front while he ate supper. My great-grandfather is believed to have burned the bridges over the Shenandoah on Jackson's order, to prevent a Yankee flanking movement.

There was a trap door in our dining room closet, which opened to a dirt-floored room with a ceiling only two or three feet high, but with no windows to betray its existence. There the family hid the silver and other valuables, as well as any Confederate soldier who suddenly found himself surrounded by the Yankees. Occasionally, I crawled around that room with a flashlight.

Family history has it that once when Marcus Bayly, my grandfather's 12-year-old half-brother, was visiting, a Yankee soldier appeared and tried to capture him at pistol point. A struggle ensued; Bayly slipped. The Yankee intruder was about to fire, when my great-grandmother threw herself on him crying, "Don't shoot my boy." He desisted and took him prisoner.

On several occasions Union General Philip Sheridan made the house his headquarters while his men plundered the Shenandoah Valley. He treated the family kindly and had his doctor attend the sick children. His visits were not a well-known part of our family tradition, however, and they were only recently discovered by my sister when she copied our great-great-grandmother's diary.

The Civil War was not the only thing that immersed our family in history. My father was interested in genealogy. The Majors believed that the founder of their family was Archbishop Mauger (pronounced Major) of Rouen, in northwest France, who was exiled to the Channel Islands by his nephew, William the Conqueror. King Henry V was thought to have given Hursley Manor to one of Mauger's descendants as a reward for his services. Eventually a Major daughter married Richard Cromwell, Oliver's son, who was briefly Lord Protector of England. There was fact, fiction, and unprovable legend in the account, but we accepted it as true. More legitimate was the claim that the Major family had been in Virginia for three centuries.

My mother's ancestors, however, had no such exalted European background, and most of them did not reach Virginia until the 18th century. An exception was the Bents, who had departed from Hampshire, England, in 1638 and had settled in Massachusetts. Two centuries later, Charles and William Bent built Bent's Fort on the Arkansas River, in southeastern Colorado. The former became the first governor of the New Mexico Territory, and the latter had two half-breed sons, who decided with some justification that the whites were more savage than the Indians. They chose to ride with the Cheyenne.

More important was the tangible evidence that surrounded me. Seventeen ancestral portraits from both sides of the family hung on the walls of Riverside, and the house was full of beautiful antique furniture. In such circumstances one would have to struggle not to be immersed in history. I was not even tempted to try.

My preoccupation with history and love of reading bore strange fruit. In the sixth grade I was asked to write a paper of a page or two on any subject. I selected the significance of the coronation of Charlemagne in 800 A.D. It was not a topic that the typical 10- or 11-year-old child would choose. When I read my paper in class, the teacher publicly asked me where I had copied it. I denied the charge indignantly, but neither the teacher nor my fellow students believed me. Before returning the papers in the next class, the teacher apologized to me before everyone. I awaited expectantly for an A when she passed out the papers, only to find a C. My numerous punctuation, spelling, and grammatical errors had proved my innocence, but at a terrible cost.

I was more fortunate the following year. A county-wide test was given to all seventh graders to determine their general knowledge. As my constant reading included the daily paper, I managed to come in first in the high school, and second in the county.

In the eighth grade I got straight As in history and science and Bs in my other subjects, except handwriting, where I was awarded a D. In the sophomore year of high school, there was no history, but I got As in mathematics and literature. Happily, handwriting ceased to be graded. My height was recorded as 68 inches and my weight as a mere 116 pounds. I was declared underweight, but passed the other health requirements. At that point my parents decided to send me to the Randolph-Macon Academy as a day student.

R.M.A. was a military prep school, but none of the day students wore uniforms or participated in drills. My father dropped me off at the foot of the hill leading up to the academy on his way to work. I had classes until one, ate lunch at a table for day students, and walked home unless I had a lab. I never got to know any of the boarding students nor participated in school activities. The one exception was in the fall of my senior year, when my father pushed me into going out for football. I was easily the worst player on the team for 125 pounders and got in on only the last play of one game, when we were so far ahead that I could do no harm. Academically, R.M.A. was better than the high school. Classes were smaller, and the all male faculty maintained strict discipline. The principal was Colonel Boggs, a large man with a chest full of World War I medals, including, I believe, the Distinguished Service Cross.

The grading system was very precise. Every month the instructor filled out a slip on each student giving his grade, the number in the class, and his class standing. As usual when confronted with a new situation, I did very badly at first, but by December I had hit my stride. History was my favorite subject, but from the third grade I also imagined myself something of a mathematician. I was soon to have a rude awakening. I graduated fourth in a class of 57 at the age of 17 in June 1938. My standing would have been acceptable had not my oldest sister, Elizabeth, finished second at the high school and given the salutatorian address. My brother, Neville, had finished first at R.M.A. five years before and had given the valedictory. Both were only 16 at the time. They were popular, well-adjusted teenagers, and I was not. Neville had played center on the R.M.A. varsity football team; I had not willingly engaged in any extra-curricular activities. I even skipped the various gatherings around graduation, but managed to make it to the degree-awarding ceremony after Colonel Boggs telephoned my parents.

I now realize that I was considered a problem child. My father had gotten the R.M.A. coach to drag me out to the football field. On another occasion I was sent to a camp near Woodstock for a week, but rejected an offer from my parents to stay longer.

One summer when I was about 15, Bim Cook, a friend, and I visited his aunt and grandfather on Cape Cod. One evening his cousin wanted the car to take a girl to a dance. His mother agreed only if I went. The cousin dragged me to the house of a girl I had casually met. She stood in the doorway while he prodded me, and I, with cast-down eyes, asked her for a date. With a choice of me or staying at home, the young lady wisely chose the latter somewhat to my relief. Bim and I lost our money playing bingo and had to get a job at a hotel washing dishes for a dollar a day. After a week's labor we were able to proceed home by bus.

On two occasions Neville took me on long camping trips in spite of the four years and more that separated us. I don't think that my parents prodded him and believe he acted out of the kindness of his heart. In August 1935, he and the Ramsey brothers planned to take a camping tour of eastern Canada. They were all about the same age, but they took me along. We visited Niagara Falls, the Thousand Islands, Ottawa, Quebec, and then headed south to a lake near Oakland, Maine, where they had a friend. We swam together in the lake during the day, and in the evenings they returned to court the girls, leaving me in the woods to guard the campsite and feed the mosquitoes. I remember with fondness a beautiful campsite we had by a stream at the foot of Mount Washington in Maine.

Then there was West Point, and New York City, where we hung our heads out of the car trying to see the top of the newly completed Empire State Building, and finally home.

Neville graduated from V.M.I. in June 1937, sold his uniforms, and bought a second-hand Ford roadster for about $50. As his job with Procter and Gamble did not begin until September, he decided to take a camping trip to California. Giles Downing, a contemporary of his, agreed to go, and they squeezed me in. Squeezed is right, as the rumble seat was used to store our gear. The car collapsed in Ohio the second day, and it took over 12 hours to fix it. From then on, it was a battle against the heat. The Dust Bowl in the Great Plains region had just passed its peak, and the temperature soared well above 100°. I still fondly remember an ice-cold watermelon we bought in Kansas for ten cents.

We saw Pikes Peak, Santa Fe, Grand Canyon, Boulder Dam, Los Angeles, Sequoia and Yosemite National Parks, and other wondrous sites.

When we left San Francisco for Salt Lake City, we traveled all night because it was so much cooler. Neville fell asleep at the wheel around dawn, and we ran off the road and turned over. The roof and windshield of the car were ruined, and a wheel was bent. We were towed to Ely, Nevada, where we wired home for $50 and got the wheel fixed. We then proceeded to Salt Lake City, Yellowstone, and home without roof or windshield to protect us from the sun and dust.

There was still some time that summer to camp with Sonny. Once he purloined some brandy from his father, and we went camping with three or four other boys at our cabin in the Fort Valley. Soon we were experimenting with the brandy. Someone bet a dollar that I could not empty a full ice tea glass without stopping. I did, and became foully drunk for the first time; but I suppose I am lucky it didn't kill me. To top it all, the rascal who made the bet never paid me the dollar.

In the summer of 1937, I got my senior lifesaving badge at Winchester, and worked that and the following summer as a lifeguard at the Front Royal Recreation Park, which was just being completed.

Throughout this period my greatest pleasure continued to be reading in our library. I expanded my interests to include Alexandre Dumas. We had a 25-volume set that chronicled his heroes from the death of King Henry

II in a tournament in 1559 until the French Revolution in 1789. Six volumes dealt with D'Artagnan and the three musketeers. My mother wondered at the wisdom of letting me read Dumas. His heroes were all brave and good swordsmen, but the ladies left something to be desired. Dumas wasted no time on lurid seduction scenes, and simply said this or that woman was a mistress. Indeed, the prurient pictures and literature to which every child is exposed today were not available in Front Royal. The *National Geographic* occasionally published an article that included the picture of a topless native woman, but that was all. The cinema was tightly censored. When Claudette Colbert exposed a stocking leg to stop a car, it was talked about for years, and Clark Gable provoked newspaper articles when he said "damn" in the movie, *Gone With The Wind*. I did stumble on a multi-volume set of Gautier in the library. I remember a sensuous description of a mummy and the rollicking story of Mademoiselle de Maupin, who ran around dressed as a man. I have since heard that there were homosexual overtones in the book, but in my ignorance they were totally lost on me. Hence, when I enrolled at V.M.I. in September 1938, I was a bashful, innocent boy devoid of athletic ability, almost totally inexperienced with firearms, and woefully lacking in self-confidence. I had never had a real date with a girl.

Chapter 2

Virginia Military Institute

I DO NOT REMEMBER ANY discussion about where I should go to college. My father had gone to V.M.I. at the age of 16, and my brother Neville had entered the Institute at the same age. He had made an enviable record, having lettered in football and boxing his "rat" (freshman) year. He was a corporal the following year, and color sergeant, then lieutenant, during his second class (junior) and first class (senior) years. He was academically distinguished throughout his cadetship, which entitled him to wear stars on his uniform. It was obvious that I could never equal his athletic record, but for all I knew I might be a good soldier. The heroes of nearly all the books I read had had military careers. The Virginia Military Institute, located in Lexington, Virginia, had been established in 1839 and was steeped in tradition. I was more than willing to give the Institute a try.

My "rat" year was a disaster, and it was only in academics that I managed to hold my own thereafter. In a school that prided itself on creating citizen soldiers and developing the whole man, this was not enough, but it never occurred to me to quit and go to another college.

In my old age I am doubly glad I stuck it out. With the rarest exceptions, V.M.I. graduates lead honest, disciplined lives and are unusually successful in their chosen professions. The most prestigious colleges and universities are far more selective in their admissions; yet many of their graduates fall by the wayside.

It was not long before I learned that the military was not my forte. The key elements of soldiering at V.M.I. were drilling and horseback riding. I soon discovered that I stood at the bottom of the class in both. Around September 24, I reported to my mother that

> I am still by far the grossest rat in my company when it comes to drilling and what is worse I am not improving. At first the worst I did was to get into the wrong squad, but tonight I got so mixed up that I marched back from mess in the file close along with the company officers. My corporal congratulated me on my rapid promotion.

The worst single incident came when the command "to the rear march" was given one day. You were supposed to reverse your direction by turning to the right or left. I still don't know which, but I did it wrong. My rifle became entangled with Andy Trzeciak's, the captain of the football team. I was nearly thrown to the ground. Some time later an old cadet remarked in his presence that I was Neville Major's brother. Trzeciak looked at me scornfully and said, "He was a man." Years later I was to learn that I was equally inept in following the intricacies of the square dance.

One explanation for my total disaster on the drill field was that I was tone deaf. My mother and oldest sister shared my handicap, but my father and other three siblings were musical. As a result I was generally out of step, and I eventually discovered that I was incapable of learning to speak a foreign language.

My disability led to more immediate troubles. One day at mess I was asked to call hogs for the edification of the upper classmen at my table. Although I was from the country, I had never heard anyone call hogs. In a sing-song voice I shouted, "Calling all hogs. Calling all hogs." In doing so, I revealed how terrible my voice was. From that time on, I was asked to sing songs for the older cadets amidst their groans and laughter. Once I was taken to our company captain's room to sing a few songs for him. He was a powerfully built man who was a star tackle on the football team.

About 30 other first classmen gathered to hear the fun. "Since then," I reported to my mother, "I have been singing and giving school yells all the time."

While the Germans were experimenting with motorized panzer tank divisions, V.M.I. trained its artillery cadets with horse-drawn World War I French 75mm guns. There was some class work in the ROTC program, but our instructors seemed to believe that the essence of becoming an officer was to have a good seat on a horse. Being poorly coordinated, this was an art I never mastered. The Army furnished the Institute with some good mounts, but most of the horses had been trained to pull artillery pieces and caissons. They followed as closely behind the horse in front of them as they could. Only a good rider could persuade them to take an independent course during riding lessons. Many of my brother rats knew good horse-flesh when they saw it. They rushed ahead and chose the best. All I knew was that a horse had four legs and that it was best to stay away from the hind two.

I remember one instance in particular that took place on a Sunday during the spring. Major John M. Fray had decided to spend the holiday afternoon teaching cadets to ride better. He was from Culpeper County as was my father, and they had been friends at the Institute. I wrote my mother:

> Saddled my horse and went into the corral to get used to his gait. Well, he threw me in five minutes. I got up and got on again. In another ten minutes he threw me a second time. A sergeant told me that I had better not take that one out, so he selected the oldest horse in the stables and told me to take him. When I tried to get on, he bucked and threw me on the ground. Someone held him while I got on and I went back to the corral. By this time I was the center of attraction but felt somewhat embarrassed.

Major Fray led the riding class down a paved road, over a bridge to a farm belonging to the Institute.

There I <u>dismounted</u> to tighten the saddle girths and when I tried to get on again, the horse threw me off. About an hour later Major Fray told us that we could ride where we pleased. There were some old cadets jumping so my horse went there. I felt in the way, but I couldn't get my horse to move on. When the old cadets left I had to get off so that I could keep the horse from following them. Then the horse wouldn't let me get back on. Finally someone came along to hold the horse for me while I got on. The horse started running towards the gate which had been left open. I couldn't stop the animal until we were halfway back to barracks. The only way I could get the horse back to the farm was to lead him. When I tried to get on again he bucked me off. I stood at the gate and waited for the class to come to hold the horse so I could get on.

Although I had obviously flunked riding, I thought that I had displayed some commendable traits: determination, persistence, and even courage in adversity. Others took a different view. "Major Fray wanted to put me in the infantry," I reported, "but I wouldn't let him." Shortly after, he invited me and a brother rat to dinner. We were entertained by his pretty, young daughter who was a splendid horsewoman. When she discovered that I was the cadet who had failed so badly in the corral, I could tell that there was no use for me to pursue the acquaintance.

V.M.I. put considerable emphasis on physical training. Those who were not good enough for rat or varsity teams were expected to win points for their company by playing intramural sports. Bull Ramey, as we called him, was in charge of the physical education program. I weighed in at 133 pounds with a height of 71-1/4 inches and a chest of 35-1/2 inches. My muscular coordination was declared to be poor, but at least Ramey reported that I had no abnormalities. By the end of the spring semester I had added 21 pounds to my weight, grown one inch, and added two more to my chest. I flunked the heavy gym, but Ramey knew that I had been a lifeguard and gave me a 10 on water training without ever seeing me swim. As a result, I received a grade of 8.0 when 7.5 was the lowest passing mark. For the year I stood 141 in a class of 199.

With such a record, nothing could be expected from my athletic prowess. I did go out for wrestling, but my long, thin body made it as easy to tie me in knots as a piece of rope. I got nowhere and soon quit. In intra-mural competition I won my first two matches to everyone's surprise, including my own. I added one or two points to the company's total in swimming and some more in ping pong, but my principal contribution was in cheering the company teams. Rats were not permitted to study or relax during intramural competition even when they were not on the team. That winter the Red Cross gave a lifesaving and water safety instructors course at the Institute that I managed to pass.

The Spartan lives we led did not bother me. The typical room was designed for four cadets, but the freshman dropout rate was very high. To compensate, the authorities admitted more students than there was space for. I ended up with four roommates in room 458. There were two desks with straight chairs on each side, one wash basin, one mirror, and no closets. We slept on cots and mattresses called "hay" that had to be stacked each morning before breakfast. Rats got up about 6 a.m., dressed, stacked their hay, and headed to the first classman's room whom they "dyked." This older cadet was usually from the rat's hometown or a friend of the family. In return for a few nominal services, the rat received advice, encouragement, and guidance. There was no need for a dean of students, and the faculty member designated as my adviser never con-tacted me.

About 7 a.m., the six companies formed and marched to breakfast. At 8 a.m., we marched to our first class. The highlight of the day came at 11 p.m. when taps sounded. Until I was 70, I was up by seven, and to this day lights go out by eleven. This was the most lasting part of my training.

The constant harassment by the upper classmen did bother me. There was never any physical abuse. One might be made to squat and push a rifle until he nearly passed out, but no rat was ever touched. There was a com-pany room where under the first sergeant's direction gross rats could thin out, push rifles, and suffer verbal abuse, and a General Committee composed of leading older cadets assigned punishments. I was sent to company room on more than one occasion, and in the spring the General Committee gave me a week's confinement and five penalty tours for some long-forgotten offense. Such experiences were not daily affairs, however.

It was the never-ending yelling and humiliating tasks such as singing that disturbed me the most.

The four-story barracks in which we all lived was ideally constructed to give upper classmen every opportunity to pester rats. Each floor was surrounded by a stoop balcony. The rats occupied the top floor. With each year, cadets worked their way down a floor until their first-class year, when they lived on the ground level and had no steps to climb. A rat was expected to march along the stoops with shoulders back, chin in, and chest out. When he came to the steps, he ran up as fast as he could. The showers, PX, and barber shop were in the basement. Thus, rats had to run the gauntlet of older cadets up three flights of steps every time they returned from class, drill, or other activity; and a fourth flight was added whenever they went to the basement. Drill, parade, and the mess hall provided further opportunities for upper-class harassment. My thoughts centered on shining shoes and the brass on my uniform, shaving, although I had nothing to shave, and in general doing everything I could to stay out of trouble. As a result my studies suffered.

Everyone took the same courses their freshman year, whether they planned to be a doctor, lawyer, or engineer. There were three semesters of mathematics, and two each of chemistry, history, English, and a foreign language. Moreover, they were all taught the same way. There was supposed to be an assignment in a textbook for each class, and students recited for a grade nearly every time they came. The usual result was boring classes but a thorough textbook knowledge of the subject. Grades were posted biweekly for all to see, and monthly grades were sent home to parents. I had had math and chemistry at Randolph-Macon Academy and should have breezed through, but my mind was set on staying out of trouble. My highest grade on my first report card other than a 9.8 in military science was a 9.2 in chemistry. I flunked trigonometry with a 7.2. By the end of the academic year, history had gained its rightful place as my best subject, but I stood only 10th in a class of 199. At least, I managed to pass trig and stood 66th in the three math courses combined. My overall class standing was only 49.

There were no class cuts, and our only holiday was two weeks at Christmas. Classes were held on Saturday mornings, and we marched to church on Sundays. Saturday and Sunday afternoons were our only free time, that is, if we had no penalty tours to walk or chores to perform for an older cadet. The degree of our confinement is illustrated in an invitation I extended to my parents to come to the homecoming football game. If they told me in advance, I could get a company permit and stay out until 9:30 Saturday night to have dinner with them. In those days V.M.I. had good football teams. We lost only to Navy and tied such teams as Virginia Polytechnic Institute, University of Virginia, and Clemson University, great disappointment being expressed that we had not defeated the first two as anticipated. In spite of the prospects of a victory, I don't remember whether my parents came.

I mention the above because it underlines how unusual it was that I or any cadet was given a weekend furlough in October. A third classman from Front Royal hated the Institute and sought every excuse to escape. He had gone to Randolph-Macon Academy as had four other members of my class. The school was about to celebrate its 50th anniversary, and our homesick student, with the support of an influential state senator and the R.M.A. authorities, persuaded the Institute to grant us a furlough to attend.

I arrived home Friday afternoon and found Blair Rogers visiting my sister Becky. Her father, Major Pleas Blair Rogers, had just been stationed at the Remount Depot about three miles out of town where horses were raised for the Army. A brass button had come off the coatee that I was to wear the following night. Blair sewed it on for me. I was greatly impressed as I believed none of my sisters had this talent. Nothing came of this initial encounter, but in the long run it was to affect my life more than any other single episode. I attended the football game Saturday afternoon and the dance that night without a date and returned to the Institute Sunday.

During the summer of 1939, I worked in the shipping department of my father's preserving plant for the minimum wage of 30 cents an hour. The work was hard and the heat was terrific as there was no air conditioning in those days. We loaded and unloaded cases of preserves, the lightest of the goods we moved. At times we had to stack 100-pound sacks of sugar, seven bags high. Barrels of fruit had to be put in cold storage. The contrast with the heat outdoors made this task worse.

I did find time to give a senior lifesaving course at the recreation park

where I had worked the summer before, but the most significant event of
the summer was that I had my first date. I dialed the Remount Depot and
in my confusion asked the operator for Major Blair's residence. Our phone
was in the upstairs hall at the head of the staircase, and my voice carried
to the rooms below. I heard the guffaws from members of my family, but
I finally got the Rogers' residence and the girl I sought.

We went to Strasburg where there was a roller-skating rink and eventually to a drug store to have an ice cream soda. I suspect that we had
several other dates, but considering that I was a rising college sophomore
and Blair was about to begin her senior year in high school, our activities
seem amazingly innocent by current standards.

My second year at the Institute was quite different from the first. The
disciplined way of life continued, but I was no longer subjected to the
many trials of a rat. Clyde Hooker, of Martinsville, had been one of my
roommates our freshman year. We decided to stick together and were
assigned one of the few three-man rooms with Al Vick of Hampton.

Clyde brought an electric phonograph and a batch of records. For the
only time in my life I began to know the names of the great bands and the
popular songs. I still remember some of the words in such favorites as
"Blueberry Hill" and "I'll Never Smile Again," but of course I never dared
to try to sing them. At least I no longer had to perform for the older cadets.
In those days the finest bands in the country were happy to play at V.M.I.
dances. There was no mass media to provide more lucrative opportunities
back then. For $5 we could attend the Friday and Saturday night dances as
well as a Saturday afternoon tea dance. Clyde constantly talked about the
beauty of the Martinsville girls, and we persuaded two of them to come to
one of the dance weekends. They brought a car and I, at least, had a fine
time.

The social event that is most firmly implanted on my mind took place
at Hollins College, which was located about 40 miles south of Lexington.
My sister Becky was a freshman, and one of Neville's V.M.I. roommates
had a sister there. They invited us to a girl-break dance early in December.
I got permission to attend, and Neville drove down from Front Royal and
picked me up. I was scared to death, and in spite of his greater age and
poise, Neville was a bit nervous. Being tone deaf, I was not much of a

dancer. To avoid being stuck, I had to rely on my non-existent gift of gab. It was necessary to find a topic of conversation that would interest the girl I was dancing with. Only if my partner smiled and seemed happy could I hope that someone would cut in. I kept a smile on my face as much to hide my fear as to attract another girl. Becky worked hard bringing up friends and introducing them to me. All went well, but I was relieved when Neville dropped me off on the way home.

The following day Becky reported to our mother, "I really never had so much fun in my life as I had last night. I was so pleased with my brothers. Neville was definitely the "belle" of the ball. . . . Russell was a close runner up for honors though." One of Becky's friends told her that I said "she was beautiful" and that I "wished we could get away from it all. . . . Can't you just see Rus saying all that?"

I remember the girl, who was far from pretty, and I said no such thing. The episode did demonstrate to me some problems that girls had when it came to dating. It caused me to sympathize with their plight more than all the activities of the feminists in the half-century that followed. I never subjected myself to such an experience again, and as far as I know, Neville never did either.

It was necessary to reciprocate by extending Becky an invitation to one of our dances. In addition to the big weekend dances with name bands such as Glenn Miller and Tommy Dorsey, there were occasional first class hops on Saturday nights. I invited her to come to one in March. I was a little worried as she was as inclined to be heavy as I was to be thin. I need not have been concerned. Her natural charm and enthusiasm carried the day. I arranged for Al Vick to cut in when I brought her on the floor and then went to work introducing her to everyone I could find. I wrote home:

> Becky got on darn good. She must have developed a gift of gab somewhere. I was sorta worried about nobody cutting in after intermission, but when I led her out on the floor four cadets cut in on her before the end of the first dance.

Her first report to mother was "Superb, stupendous, colossal, magnificent." Thereafter, she often appeared at V.M.I. dances on her own. Family solidarity had paid off.

My father and brother had majored in civil engineering; but cognizant of my impractical nature, I decided to take the liberal arts curriculum. I thought I was less likely to fail as a lawyer than as a road builder. Actually, the course requirements were not too different in the third class year. Liberal artists were required to take physics, but we had a choice of geology, biology, or calculus rather than being required to take the last.

Without the trauma of being a "rat" my freshman year, my grades improved. I made the honor list on the first monthly report and every time thereafter while I was a cadet, with one exception. I recently learned, when I went over material to write this chapter, that General Charles Evans Kilbourne, the superintendent, looked over the reports that were sent home and often commented on the better ones. On my first report, he wrote: "A fine record of studies. I hope and believe he will reduce his demerits." I had already been given 22, while the preceding year I had received only 3, and those in the last week or two after we had ceased to be rats.

The most memorable course I took that year was a survey of English literature taught by "Dodo" Dillard. Dodo was in the process of completing his dissertation at Harvard and had joined the Institute faculty the year before. He had spent most of that year teaching German, and this was the first time he had an opportunity to preside over the course that was to make him famous.

I don't know whether Dodo had any interpretative ability, but he had a photographic mind. Once he read a sonnet he had never seen before and repeated it back to the class with only one slip. The two things he brought to the course were an unbridled enthusiasm and the willingness to say the most outrageous things. On more than one occasion he declared, "When in doubt, don't consult the dictionary, consult me."

Unhappily, Dodo thought that we could read as fast and memorize poetry as easily as he did. He produced a reading list so long that if we read a book a day, we would not complete it during the term. Also, there were many lines of poetry we had to memorize as well. We argued long and hard against his requirements and finally got the reading assignment reduced to 700 pages a week. I did very well the first semester, but by the second my complaints had convinced him that I never would be a scholar. I stood fifth in a class of 26 for the year. I will say there was never a boring minute in his class, and he was to become the most beloved teacher the

Institute ever had. I am sure he lowered his requirements for his students a little later, or he would never have won so many adherents.

At times, I got monthly grades as high as 9.7 in physics and 9.9 in calculus. I began to have delusions of beating the engineers at their own game. They referred to liberal arts majors as "hay hounds" and regarded us as inferiors. Unhappily, I got some mediocre monthly grades in physics and collapsed on the final exam in calculus in the spring. The last was especially disappointing. I generally did as well or better on examinations as I did in classroom work. Both Colonel Mayo and Colonel Byrnes, the math professors, asked me how I did when I turned in my paper. I must have disappointed them as much as I did myself. For the year I stood 18th in physics and 32nd in calculus in a class of 144. My only first stand came in English history where I competed against the other 25 liberal artists.

Sonny Smith had entered V.M.I. that fall. He was as "gross" a rat as I had been, but the hazing of the older cadets never phased him. He also failed to make the grade academically, but he remained happy, cheerful, and always friendly.

After I had worked part of the summer in my father's plant, Sonny and I took off in a secondhand wreck he had bought. We visited his brother rat Frank Williams, who lived near the Georgia coast. We went to Sea Island, which was then unspoiled, and sailed in boats up and down along the hard-packed beach. I had a date with an attractive girl named Virginia Bell. Fired by my poetic instincts, I sent her a postcard after we left saying:

Virginia Bell
Is as cute as hell.

So much for all the literary culture I had recently imbibed from Dodo Dillard.

We also visited Peyton Thompson in Waynesboro, Georgia, where his family was having a barbecue. Peyton was a rosy-cheeked, quiet boy who was to lose his life four years later as an infantry officer in Normandy. Finally, we stopped by Martinsville for a few delightful days with the Hookers.

The most momentous event that summer was Margaret Bargeron's visit to Riverside after our return. She was a classmate of Becky's at Hollins and lived in Chevy Chase, Maryland. Her father was an adviser and leg man for Wendell Willkie, the Republican candidate for president in 1940. It is hard to imagine two people who had less in common. Margaret was a highly sophisticated Washingtonian whose life centered on night clubs and restaurants. I remained the awkward country boy. But opposites sometimes attract. I became a frequent visitor to Hollins that fall.

In addition to Sunday afternoons, second classmen were permitted to stay out until 10 p.m. one Saturday night a month. I invited Margaret to the ceremonial ring figure the weekend after Thanksgiving. It was the most important dance in a cadet's career because he wore the formal mess jacket for the first time. His date placed his class ring on his finger, and they kissed under a flowered arch as was the tradition.

During the Christmas holidays I visited Fred Jones and his relatives in Alexandria, Virginia. Fred was from Phoenix and had roomed with Clyde and me our rat year. He had dropped out in our third class year, but had returned in the fall of 1940 and was sharing a four-man room with Clyde, Al, and me. His home in Arizona was much too far away to go for a two-week holiday in those days, and Fred remained in the East with relatives. From this friendly base, we night clubbed with Margaret and his date.

By the New Year, our relationship had begun to cool. I took her out to dinner at the swank Roanoke Hotel after school started in January, but to no avail. I terminated the courtship by returning her picture and never saw her thereafter. For a time I was disconsolate, but as spring drew near my thoughts turned to Blair Rogers.

Academically, my second class should have been a huge success, as I had satisfied all my math and science requirements, but I picked up German to replace them. I found German to be a more difficult and a less interesting subject. At the end of the first semester, General Kilbourne noted on my report card that I and one other cadet were "'neck and neck' for first stand." By June I had lost out to Tommy Wilson. However, I stood first in American history and second in four other subjects, but it was not enough. Most surprising, I was tenth in military science for the year in a class that had shrunk to 143, but it was all because of the class, not the drills.

At V.M.I., cadets marched to church every Sunday. The nearest was the Episcopal, but it held the longest services. The most distant, a Reformed Presbyterian Church, held the shortest services. Although a nominal Episcopalian, I often chose the latter. On April 27, even its services seemed too much. I dropped out as we marched through town, was caught, and received 10 demerits, 2 weeks confinement to barracks, and 15 penalty tours. I spent my May weekends walking. But in spite of the 10 demerits, I ended the academic year with only 65, 2 less than the year before, when I had escaped confinement completely.

The summer after my second class year was devoted largely to ROTC camp. Artillerymen were sent to Fort Bragg, North Carolina. A unit from Duquesne University was equipped with the new 105mm truck-drawn howitzers. True to tradition, the Institute clung to her horses and the 75mm gun. No matter the Germans had already overrun Poland and France.

Students at Duquesne also created a better impression. They constituted the small percentage of the student body who were truly interested in the military, and this was their first chance to play soldier. The V.M.I. contingent included many like me who were devoid of military aspirations. We had been playing soldier for three years. Now the time had come to play, period. We had nicknamed our senior officer "Happy" Heiner because he never smiled. We called theirs "Flutterballs." Flutterballs' students treated him with the utmost reverence. Colonel Heiner enjoyed no such deference, although he was a nice enough man.

The Army was still trying to save money in training exercises. A 37mm gun was mounted on our 75mm gun for training purposes because its shells cost less. It mattered not that they kicked up so little dust that it was difficult to adjust fire. Long debates and explanations took place before each round was fired. We were constantly admonished to do our best because the U.S. was certain to be involved in the war now raging in Europe. It went in one ear and out the other. I learned little or nothing during those six weeks.

Two episodes from that summer do stick in my mind. In field exercises, the cadets played the various roles in a battery from captain to cannoneer. On this particular occasion, I was messenger bugler number one. In this capacity, I was sitting on my horse by the battery when a gun went off. So did my horse. He charged down the road at a full gallop. We had gone about a mile before I was able to turn him around. When I got back to the battery feeling very proud of myself because I had not fallen off, I was accosted by Mac Tabb. He was from the heart of the Virginia horse country, and had been the captain of the polo team and the master of the hounds when he was a cadet. Now a second lieutenant, he was not likely to be sympathetic. He looked at me with the utmost scorn and said, "Well, you have decided to rejoin us, Mr. Major."

I then realized that if I went into battle on a horse, I would win the Medal of Honor posthumously if my mount decided to charge the enemy, or I would be shot as a deserter if he chose to go the other way. Neither prospect was too pleasing. The solution to my dilemma, I decided, was to fall off immediately regardless of which way the horse went. After all, I was a past master of the art and had hit the ground more often than any other man in my class, and without serious mishap.

The second episode occurred on the pistol range. I had never held a pistol in my life and had no natural talent. The target was a man-shaped object whose side was presented to the marksman. When a rope was pulled, the target turned toward him and the cadet fired. Try as I would, I never hit the target. The ultimate ignominy occurred when my bullet hit the rope that ran along the ground to turn the target. *The Bomb*, our yearbook, which usually found only nice things to say about graduating cadets, called me the "terror on the pistol range." I was disgraced and felt only joy when summer camp came to an end.

Officers were to have qualified with the pistol before being sent overseas. In the spring of 1944, someone in our battalion headquarters noticed that I had never done so. Along with a few other delinquent officers, I was once more taken to the pistol range. This time the rope went unharmed and a few of my stray bullets hit the target, but not often enough to qualify. My failure was overlooked. I accompanied my battalion to England and then to Normandy without more ado.

I need hardly say that I was a private during my entire stay at the Institute, but when I reported in September 1941, I was a first classman. No one was over me except the officers, and they were my brother rats. By then, Blair Rogers and I had become interested in each other. Unhappily for me, she had elected to go north to Vassar College rather than attend one of the nearby girls' colleges. I was left to wander rather aimlessly at a time when I had a little more freedom.

First classmen were permitted to have one weekend furlough a month. I don't remember what I did on the first one, but in mid-November I took Hattie Lu, Blair's sister who had recently graduated from Vassar, to College Park to see V.M.I. defeat the University of Maryland by a score of 27 to 0. I don't know what I had planned for December, but it made no difference. First class furloughs were canceled after the attack on Pearl Harbor on December 7, 1941.

We turned on our radio after we returned from lunch that Sunday afternoon and learned of the attack. At first the news was garbled. There was even a report that our Pacific fleet had sailed out to meet the Japanese. I received a telegram from my father telling me not to enlist. General Kilbourne summoned the corps to the Jackson Memorial Hall and issued the same instructions. The Army would call us when we were needed. It had never occurred me to jump to the colors, and so far as I know, none of my classmates had any such thoughts either. We were less gung ho than our parents. General Kilbourne was obeyed without even a secret demur.

General Kilbourne was the most distinguished-looking man I had ever seen. Tall, erect, with snow-white hair, he was every inch a soldier. He had graduated second in the V.M.I. class of 1894 and had entered the Army at the beginning of the Spanish-American War. During his long career he had become the first man ever to hold all three of the highest military decorations: the Medal of Honor, the Distinguished Service Cross, and the Distinguished Service Medal. He had retired in 1936 as a major general at a time when only the chief of staff held a higher rank, and he had become the Institute's sixth superintendent the following year.

The Sam Brown belt on which officers carried their swords had just become optional. When asked whether we should buy one, the General replied that an officer should be clearly distinguishable in battle. I later saw officers put tape over their bars in combat so that they could not be recognized. The current camouflage uniforms fail to distinguish between officers and men. Again one is struck by how much things have changed since World War I.

Once General Kilbourne described how he and others had fortified Corregidor so that the Japanese could never take it. He was later proved wrong, because he neglected to consider how poorly prepared MacArthur's troops were for combat. They were defeated by an inferior number of Japanese and retreated so rapidly that most of their supplies never reached Bataan. Then, too, MacArthur had lost his air support hours after Pearl Harbor.

If General Kilbourne was mistaken about the outcome of the Philippines campaign, he nevertheless had our best interests at heart. He was determined that we would graduate before the West Pointers so that we would have an earlier date of rank. To justify an early graduation, he terminated the first classmen's monthly furloughs and canceled the spring hike and final examinations. Thus, we lost the privileges we had so long dreamed of and were expected to concentrate on our studies.

I don't remember being inspired to greater effort because of the war, but the first semester of my senior year was my best at the Institute. I stood first in four of the five liberal arts courses and fifth among my 137 classmates in economics. The second semester was less spectacular, because I proved to be as poor a student in my public speaking class as I had been in German.

My non-academics did not fare so well, although I did have one triumph. In riding class we were required to tie up the reins on our horse, hold our hat over our eyes, kick the beast, and go over a jump. One brother rat fell and broke his arm, but my mount and I stuck together. It was my first success as a horseman, but such things were becoming less important. The war brought promotions and reassignment to most of the Regular Army officers. Major Basil P. Cooper arrived, a Reserve officer who was more interested in fire-direction centers than in a horseman's seat.

Clyde and I met two girls from Fairfax Hall, a two-year girls' college. We invited them to a first class hop on March 22. Cadets were allowed an hour to escort their dates back to their downtown hotel. If one sought to go by taxi, he had to wait his turn. If he elected to walk, his date had to negotiate the sidewalks in her evening dress and high heels. I don't remember which my date and I did, but when we reached the hotel, we spent some time talking in the lobby. I arrived back at barracks a half-hour late and found that our room had been checked. I had to report myself as absent, for which I received five demerits and a week's confinement to barracks. Immediately thereafter I heard from Blair. She was home from Vassar on spring vacation and could catch a ride to V.M.I. with Sonny Smith the following weekend. I had to report that I would still be under confinement. The repercussions of this event have not ceased over a half-century later.

One weekend in early May just as classes were coming to an end, I decided to explore a cave near Lexington with George Rhea and Spencer Hockaday. George had replaced Fred Jones as our roommate, when Fred had decided to enter dental school rather than return to V.M.I. Spencer was my wrestling companion, a sport he especially enjoyed, because he always won. Sonny Smith and I had explored Allen's Cave just outside of Front Royal, and I had no hesitation in tackling another cavern. This was especially true, as Allen's Cave had recently been opened to the public and renamed the Skyline Caverns. Surely the Lexington cave could be no more challenging than one that was now lighted that people paid to see.

We had only two flashlights, and the batteries were weak in one of them. Nevertheless, we intrepid explorers entered the cave around 3 p.m. I reported to my mother,

> [We] climbed . . . down to the bottom without paying any particular attention as to where we were going. When we got there, one flashlight was completely out and the other was weak. On the way back we took the wrong turn somewhere and couldn't find our way out. We crawled around here and there over high ledges, beside underground rivers, and over deep ravines where if we slipped we would fall at least fifty feet. When our flashlight went out, we would sit and wait for it to recharge itself enough for us to go on.

Luckily, we were at a military school and were reported absent at taps.

Colonel Fray called for volunteers, and he led the rescue mission himself.
They found us sometime after midnight.

> They had all kinds of equipment with them such as ropes, a
> string to keep them from getting lost, etc. . . . . We were nearly
> frozen as we had gotten wet, and the cave was very cold and
> muddy. . . . At present we are being razzed by all the barracks,
> but I reckon we deserve it. They call us the three dumb cave
> men.

Colonel Fray took us to a little diner that stayed open all night and bought
us hamburgers.

The Bomb said that I was "brilliant at book learning," meaning that I
was dumb at everything else. I was happy that the yearbook had already
gone to press, and this incident could not be added to my description as
the "terror of the pistol range."

My troubles were not yet over. Someone had thrown a spit devil on the
first stoop. Impulsively and without thinking, I put my foot on it, creating
a resounding crack. The sentinel in the courtyard demanded my name, and
soon I was in the commandant's office. The usual punishment for setting
off firecrackers included a week's confinement. If imposed, I could not go
to the final dance, and I had a date. I asked if I could see the superintendent as soon as possible, so if necessary I could break the engagement.
The wheels of justice moved rapidly, and I was ushered into General
Kilbourne's presence that same day. It was my only one-on-one meeting
with that distinguished gentleman. I tried to explain that I had acted on
impulse and had intended no harm, a very lame excuse. I was sure that he
had heard that three cadets had been lost in a cave a few days before, and
I feared he also knew that I was one of "the three dumb cave men." The
whole episode seemed so stupid now. I watched the General's face. He
fought courageously to suppress a smile; but in spite of all his efforts, his
face twitched. At length he accepted my lame excuse. The dance was on.
Perhaps my grades influenced him a little. More important, I suspect that
the authorities were inclined to be a little lenient because we were about
to participate in a terrible war.

That my last surmise is correct is supported by an event that had taken
place a month or two earlier. Hockaday and I had bought a secondhard car
our second class year and stored it in a garage near the Institute. It was a

semi-wreck, and the fuel line was partly stopped up. We had to rush down hills to get the momentum to go up the other side with an assist from the limited amount of fuel that reached the engine. The car was adequate to go up and down the valley visiting girls' schools, but I don't know that we had ever tried to take it over a mountain before. To own or drive a car was a serious offense, but one pretty April Sunday afternoon I drove through Lexington.

The next day in history class, Colonel Fuller compared the way things used to be with the way they were now. Then he added, "These days young men like to ride around Sunday afternoon in cars, don't they, Mr. Major?" He never reported me. Perhaps he was generous because he was not much of a disciplinarian in spite of graduating from the Citadel and having taught at Texas A&M, but I suspect the prospect of war had something to do with it.

The Jackson-Hope Medal also hung in doubt until near the very end. A wealthy English gentleman and Confederate sympathizer named Hope had taken the lead in raising money to erect a statue of Stonewall Jackson in Richmond. The money left over was given to V.M.I., and beginning in 1877, gold Jackson-Hope Medals were awarded to the two cadets with the highest academic average over the four years. Briefly, beginning in 1935, the award was given to the first distinguished graduate in each of the four curricula: civil engineering, electrical engineering, chemistry, and liberal arts. The question was whether I had been able to pull up my rat year grades enough to be a distinguished graduate. The two preceding years no liberal artist had, and that medal had not been awarded. Eleven semesters of laboratory science and mathematics were more than many lovers of history and English could recover from. My chances had taken a blow when it was decided not to count the final spring semester because there were no examinations.

In the same letter in which I had told my parents about the cave episode, I had informed them that I doubted if I would be a distinguished graduate. I failed to mention the Jackson-Hope Medal and sincerely believed that they never thought there was a chance. In this I was wrong. Later, I found that my father had calculated my grade average month after month, and I suspect that he had been in touch with one or two members of the faculty.

The suspense ended when Colonel Fuller remarked in one of our last classes that there would be a liberal arts medalist that year. By specializing, I had managed to slip by. Either Clyde Hooker, who came in second, or Tommy Wilson, who was third, could have easily beaten me, but they had had many other interests.

All was finally in place. Anne Morrissey came from Hollins to attend the dance on May 14, and my parents drove down from Riverton. Graduation took place the following morning, May 15, 1942. Clyde had been elected to give the valedictory address and did a fine job. The Jackson-Hope Medals were awarded next. When my name was called, I marched up on the platform and was handed the gold medal by Lieutenant General K. E. Smart of the Australian army. I returned a few minutes later to receive the Bothwell Graham Medal for standing first in liberal arts. My parents had hoped that I would get the first medal, but they were not sure. The second came as a complete surprise. On the way home that afternoon I sat on the back seat. I heard my father murmur to my mother who was driving, "Who would believe that a son of mine would get the Jackson-Hope Medal?"

It was the first thing I had ever done that was right.

Chapter 3

Forts Bragg and Sill

E ARRIVED HOME IN TIME for dinner on Friday, May 15. We new second lieutenants from Virginia had orders to report to Fort Monroe ten days later for physical examinations. The need for our services had been too great to give us a decent vacation, but the examination period moved at a very relaxed pace. It was not until June 3 that we were found to be physically qualified, and those of us in the artillery were ordered to proceed to Fort Bragg, North Carolina, to receive a month's basic instruction.

We graduated on July 11, 1942, and I was ordered with five other members of my V.M.I. class to report to Fort Sill, Oklahoma, on July 22 to attend Battery Officer Course (BOC) 65. There was time for a brief vacation. I headed home.

Blair Rogers was there, home for her summer vacation from Vassar. Her family's situation was changing drastically. Major Rogers was soon to become a brigadier general and would command the London, England, Base Section. Her mother had rented an apartment wing on the home of Ed Stokes in Front Royal and was boarding their horses in a stable in the town.

Blair and I renewed our courtship. Once we went riding in the foothills of the Blue Ridge Mountains just below the Skyline Drive. I acquitted myself satisfactorily; there were no mishaps. Perhaps the hours spent learning to ride at the Institute would be useful after all. The Rogers were avid horsemen, and Blair was a splendid rider, having participated in fox hunts and horse shows.

All too soon it was time to leave. I rode by train to Oklahoma City and by bus on to Lawton and Fort Sill.

There were 30 lieutenants in my section of BOC 65, including Ed Swain and Jack Whitmore from V.M.I. I also came to know William Macauley from Salt Lake City quite well. Together we moved from one course to another. Those who flunked an exam had to repeat the course. "Motors" was the first, followed by "Matériel." Luckily, the tests were written. If they had turned me loose on a truck with a monkey wrench, I would be in school yet. At least the only horses on the post were for riding.

There was a story going around that there had been some experiments with a mule to see whether a 37mm gun could be fired from its back. The fuse had been lit and had begun to crackle. The mule turned around to see what the noise was, and the shell flew in the direction of the high-ranking officers, who had gathered to witness the experiment. Whether the story was true or false, the artillery branch was now hell-bent on motorizing everything it could. I was relieved that my fate would not depend on which way my horse chose to run when a gun was fired.

The five-week Gunnery course came next — the first one I truly enjoyed. After it was over, we moved to a new barracks in which the walls went to the ceiling, and there was a closet in each room.

We began a week's course on Communications and the use of telephones, radios, and secret codes, which I found difficult. A first lieutenant, one of Neville's brother rats who had taught us at V.M.I., had flunked both it and Gunnery. I laid the groundwork for excusing any failure I might encounter by informing my mother that the lieutenant had taught me all the gunnery, communications, and tactics I knew before I came here.

At some point, we spent a day or two on Mess Management taught by a middle-aged second lieutenant. I suspect he had been a Mess sergeant who had been made an officer to teach a course that no one else wanted.

He kept a C and a K ration on his desk regardless of the topic discussed. The reason became apparent when a colonel came in to inspect. Without a pause he dropped the subject he was teaching and began to explain the contents of the two rations I was to come to know so well. It was the one thing he was good at, and he wanted to put his best foot foremost. One comment he made stuck in my mind more than anything else that occurred while I was at Fort Sill: "Hot foods should be served hot and cold foods should be served cold," he boldly proclaimed. The thought appealed to him so much that he repeated it. I have never forgotten this great culinary lesson.

The last and longest subject we took was Tactics, which included everything we had not already studied as well as the practical application of previous course work. The key was the Regimental Standard Operating Procedures (RSOP), a guide to maneuvers where students assumed various roles for usually half a day. On one of the first, our battery performed very badly. The instructor cussed us out even more vehemently than we deserved, as Lieutenant Colonel Draper had been watching the whole performance. We changed positions for the next maneuver as previously planned. William Macauley assumed the role of captain and I the executive. Thoroughly chastened, our fellow lieutenants determined to do their best regardless of how insignificant their roles. Macauley made the reconnaissance, and I brought the battery into the new position and prepared it to fire. To Lieutenant Colonel Draper it seemed like a magical transformation accomplished by the two new officers, Macauley and Major. In fact, if we had commanded the first time and the first two officers the last, they would have received the accolades and we would have been disgraced. The good colonel did not seem to realize that a team of recent ROTC graduates could do it correctly if they took the trouble, and the thorough lacing out of the first group had inspired them to do so. Our success was to have a profound effect on our military careers.

We did not have much time for recreation while in school. Many Saturday afternoons were taken up with artillery demonstrations, and we had to do a little studying also. I did take in an occasional movie on the post — *Mrs. Miniver*, the most enjoyable. We also went swimming in the pool and occasionally had Sunday dinner at the Officers Club. Clyde Hooker and Ed Swain had cars, and we sometimes strayed to Lawton and farther afield.

On October 2, our class of BOC 65 had a farewell banquet at the Officers Club. The eight of us from V.M.I. and one of our instructors who had graduated in 1923 "got together and sang school songs and gave a few yells much to the displeasure of all the other guests."

Our biggest occupation as graduation neared was to speculate on our next assignment. A new class graduated each week, and we were almost as interested in where their orders sent them as they were. On the Friday before graduation, we were told that most of us would be sent back to the replacement center from which we had come to await reassignment.

I planned to catch a ride back with Ed Swain. We hoped to reach Lexington Saturday in time to see the football game. Then I would catch a bus home that night if there was one. If not, I would arrive on Sunday for a ten-day leave. We expected to receive our orders on Tuesday, but had to go on battalion maneuvers that night. I was to be the executive of one of the batteries and anticipated firing many rounds.

On Tuesday, October 12, I received orders to report to Bragg. I wired home: "Temporarily stationed at Bragg. Home Saturday night or Sunday."

Everything seemed set, but when I returned from maneuvers around noon Wednesday, I found that my orders had been changed. I was assigned to teach Tactics at the Field Artillery School, at Fort Sill. I tried to get a leave from the school so that I could go home with Swain. At first they said yes, and I packed my things in his car. Then I was told there would be a day's delay. Swain could not wait, so I abandoned the idea of a leave in the hope I could get a longer one later. I wired home again to say that I could not come.

That Saturday I poured out my frustration to my parents in a long, barely coherent letter.

Of all the things I feared most, teaching here was it, and tactics is the worst subject to teach. It includes administration, law, and logistics as well. All of them are indefinite and require a lot of experience to teach. And to top it off I am stuck here for at least a year. They took five members of the BOC and officer candidate school classes to be instructors, and I had to be one of them. There were at least 550 all together.

Several experienced heads tried to console me. I was assured of at least two promotions during my assignment, they said, but the thought of being a captain in nine or ten months was not enough to compensate for the loss of a leave and a job that no officer without field experience could hope to perform satisfactorily. I completed the letter the next day: "Will never understand how they picked me to stay here." I was wrong. I do understand now. The other officer assigned to Tactics was William Macauley. Colonel Draper was one of the highest ranking officers in the school. He thought that we had miraculously transformed a sloppy battery into an efficient unit on that fateful day.

There was nothing to do but to make the best of it. Clyde Hooker and another brother rat, Thee Gilliam, had come to the school a week before I did, and the former had been assigned to School Troops and the latter to Tactics. Clyde had a car, and he generously hauled his footbound brother rats around. He lived in a permanent building on the old post. Thee and I each had a small room in a new frame structure.

Around the end of January, we decided to combine our quarters into a bedroom and a living room. We didn't buy any decent furniture, but the arrangement was more livable. At that time, the brother rats who had not yet come to Sill were sure to be sent there sooner or later if they were in the artillery. On the Saturday I wrote the bad news to mother, Clyde, Thee, and I went to a V.M.I. party at the polo club, and that Sunday we attended Joe Perkins' wedding. He had just been sent to the post to take the three-month Battery Officers Course. His bride turned out to be a wonderful cook. The V.M.I. contingent had Thanksgiving dinner at their place with all the traditional trimmings. We enjoyed the Perkins' hospitality so often that five of us chipped in to buy them two excellent suitcases for Christmas.

It took me a long time to become reconciled to my assignment. School had ended on a Wednesday, and my first class was the following Monday. The topic was aircraft defense.

I wrote my mother:

Don't know an earthly thing about it. Probably have a Major
sitting in on it too, which won't help. I have a two hour lecture
on logistics — another subject on which I am 100% ignorant.

Before the month had ended, I was writing that "I have about decided
to insult a colonel to get out of this place. Hear that if they don't like you
they will let you go."

The source of my unhappiness was that most of the other instructors
with whom I shared a large office were college graduates who had spent a
few months in the Army before being sent to Officer Candidate School.
They had been teaching for a while and were able to incorporate their
troop experience into their teaching experience.

I have always been slow to adjust to new situations and was clearly the
least confident and the most ignorant officer in the group. It did not help
matters when I was promoted to first lieutenant on November 4, less than
three weeks after I had been assigned to the school. Obviously, I had been
recommended for promotion almost immediately because of my date of
rank at a time when abler and more experienced officers were still second
lieutenants. They resented it, and I was embarrassed. I would have kept it
secret for a while if it had been possible. As it was, I received some criticism from my superiors for taking three or four days to replace my first
lieutenant's gold bars with the silver ones of a second lieutenant.

We had the 24th and the 25th off for Christmas, which fell on a Thurs-
day and a Friday, but we had to be present to teach that Saturday. Nevertheless, Macauley and I decided to go to Dallas. We got off Wednesday in
time to catch an early evening bus and arrived at Dallas at 1 a.m. We
checked in at the Hotel Adolphus and slept late.

On our way out of the hotel after breakfast, we met two women with
several empty bottles in their arms. They were employees at a millinery
store where a Christmas Eve party was being held and wanted to exchange
their "dead soldiers" for live ones. We readily agreed and proceeded with
them to a large room over the store where the party was in full swing.
Ham, turkey, and all kinds of food and drinks were provided as well as
dance music.

I reported to my mother that I had met a switchboard operator "who was one of the cutest girls I ever saw. I immediately hooked up with same and spent a very enjoyable afternoon with her between the dance floor and the eggnog bowl."

Mac found a girl of mediocre appearance — for once I had come out on top. We went to a movie after the party. The girls had to leave around 8 p.m. for another engagement, but not before I had extracted my date's name, Evelyn B., and her address.

After a sumptuous dinner, we went to midnight services at the Cathedral of the Sacred Heart. The bishop officiated, and the ceremony was spectacular. Mac was a Catholic, which had dictated our choice of churches. If anything, he was younger than I was, but he already had a master's degree in history. As we left the Cathedral, some kindly Texans asked us to Christmas dinner, but we had to catch the train that morning back to the post.

Fort Sill is the coldest place on earth when the wind blows out of the north. As artillery observers have to take up position on hilltops, their lot is a miserable one. In mid-January 1943, the temperature had dropped to below zero on a day we held a field exercise. My immediate supervisor, a lieutenant colonel, played the role of battalion commander and crouched shivering at the crest of a hill. My job was to bring the students who were acting as battery commanders to him to receive their orders. I halted the students' jeeps at the foot of the hill and had them run up to receive their orders. It was tactically sound, because the enemy could not see our cars; but it was poor politics. The frozen colonel would have preferred for me to have brought the jeeps almost to the crest of the hill at full speed. My solution and the school's coincided, so I escaped immediate reprimand.

The other instructors and I were to accompany our respective batteries to critique how well they went into position. The colonel said we could bring our students in early, but mine did a sloppy job. I kept them out until the exercise was complete. When I got back to the office, he sarcastically asked me where I had been and if I had enjoyed my run up the hill. I answered that I thought he had given us permission but not ordered us to come in early. From that time on, I knew that my name was "mud," especially since I had proved him wrong on a fine point of military law a few days before. He wasn't such a bad fellow in some ways. I am sure I was a trial to my superiors, but his next action was to turn down my request for a leave in mid-March.

Then the blow fell. Around February 10, I was summoned by Colonel Knapp, our overall supervisor, who directed me to report to Colonel Smith, the head of the New Division Officers Course (NDOC). I was being kicked sideways and a little bit upstairs. Whenever a new division was formed, the captains and higher-ranked Artillery officers were sent to Fort Sill for a month's refresher course. The NDOC department was short-handed and had asked for another officer. I was the chosen one, selected obviously because it was the most convenient way to get rid of me. At least they had to extol my virtues to get the NDOC to take me, and I departed with an excellent efficiency rating.

The course lasted only a month, and we refreshed the incoming officers on everything the school taught from the obvious Gunnery and Tactics to the not-so-obvious Drill and Marksmanship. In some classes the senior and junior officers were separated — my responsibilities lay with the latter.

Colonel Smith, the head of the school, was a tall, thin, low-key, West Point graduate. Most of the faculty were captains or majors who had had civilian careers and were in their thirties. I was the only lieutenant, except for a supply officer who outranked me by many months. I also was the youngest and most inexperienced member of the faculty, but since I was the lowest-ranking, that was what I was supposed to be. I was content and liked my new colleagues; however, the new assignment meant a further postponement of any leave.

I wrote my mother that I

can't believe that last week my greatest and most secret ambition was to go through the NDOC as a student when my year
was up here, and my only fear was that I wouldn't know enough
to pass. Now I am to teach it. Doubt if I last very long.

Clyde, Thee, and I caught the Saturday afternoon train to Dallas, and I had a date with Evelyn, a wonderful way to celebrate the events of the week.

My new assignment meant that I had to get up early to catch a truck to the old post where our school was situated, and I had a two-mile walk home. For the first few weeks, I was instructed to attend classes and learn all I could. Every menial chore was also assigned to me and included keeping the duty roster. I reported the following to my mother:

> Lieutenant Major: "Er, Major Martin, I have you down for the job of herding students at the demonstration this Saturday afternoon."
> Major Martin: "Lieutenant, I am afraid I won't be able to take my turn this time. I have some business to attend to. Wouldn't you like to do it this time for me?"
> Lieutenant Major (with clicking heels and falling face): "Thank you, Sir. I'll be glad to, Sir."

On a Friday afternoon shortly after joining the NDOC staff, I was sent out onto the range with two men and twelve rockets equipped with parachutes to participate in an experiment. When I received an order by radio from some officers several miles away, I was to set off a rocket; the parachute would open and the officers would survey it, thereby discovering my location. At first all went well, but the parachute failed to open on the seventh and eighth rockets. The range was covered with tall, dead grass, and a strong wind was blowing. On reaching the ground, the hot rockets started a fire that we were unable to put out, and several thousand acres were burned. My superior growled, "Built a big fire, Lieutenant." I became known as a pyromaniac.

Nearly every Saturday afternoon there was an artillery demonstration, and one of my jobs was to lead OCS students to the side of a hill where they could watch. A key aspect was to show how artillery fire could be massed by a fire-direction center. In a matter of seconds, shells from the 16 howitzers of a battalion or even from all 4 battalions in a division could be placed on a target. It was a spectacular display at a cost of tens of thousands of dollars, but I could not help remembering how the year before we had saved money in ROTC camp by firing one 37mm shell at a time from a gun mounted on a 75mm gun. It had taken the Army a year to forget its frugal habits, and I fear that over a half-century later, it has not rediscovered them.

There had been no problem marching the students to their proper place, but then I was supposed to get the colonels and majors of the new divisions there as well. Division artillery was commanded by a one-star general, or by a colonel who anticipated getting a star shortly. I asked each of them to have OCS officers marched to the proper place. They each turned to a colonel and told him to take care of it. My officers cut a better appearance than theirs. I was beginning to learn.

One day I was instructed to take the battery commanders out to the rifle range to show them the approved way to teach their men to shoot their carbines. Since I had never fired a carbine in my life, I felt a little foolish, but all went well. Thank the Lord, it was not a pistol that I was to demonstrate.

Sometimes the war games were more fun. Once I was the commander of an infantry regiment. I was equipped with a driver and radio operator but no staff or troops. I established my command post under a tree, where the artillery liaison officers reported to me for instructions. As in real life, they were majors and I a lieutenant; we could see the humor of the situation. They were careful to call me colonel, and I acted the part as best as I could.

There was also instruction in the classroom. In mid-April when I was teaching foreign maps, Colonel Smith and Majors Anderson and Hunt also attended, and occasionally I had other visitors. I now realize that I had been six months in grade, and my superiors were trying to decide whether to recommend me for promotion. I was none too sure of Colonel Smith. There was an officers' baseball league in which we had to compete. He was as awkward on the playing field as I was. One afternoon when I was umpire, he hit the ball. I called him out without noticing that the first baseman did not have his foot on the base. The Colonel was a good sport and said nothing, but it was the only time in the team's history he came anyway near to getting a hit.

Furthermore, the rumor was rampant that Army Ground Forces had decreed that no one was to be promoted to captain who had not had troop duty. Or to put it another way, no one was to be promoted more than once during their year at the school. Nevertheless, in April Major Hunt "practically told me that I had been recommended for a captaincy," but the rumor was all too true. I was frozen as a lieutenant as long as I remained at Fort Sill. I could at least take some satisfaction knowing that my superiors had tried. For a brief moment, I wasn't the junior officer on our staff. A lieutenant with troop duty I outranked was assigned to us, but he was soon promoted to captain.

I did have one interesting experience about this time. It had been decided to activate a new airborne division, and its artillery officers were to attend glider school at the Laurinburg-Maxton Airbase in North Carolina from May 24 to June 4. I was one of three officers from the post who were told to attend.

The rivers were flooded, and the two of us who traveled together had to go by train via New Orleans and Atlanta. There were long layovers in both cities. We ate at Antoine's, saw the cathedral and other sites in New Orleans, and hired a taxi to drive us around Atlanta. It was my first visit to either city. Little did I know that I was to spend most of my life in the latter.

Much of our time at the school was devoted to learning how to load 75mm howitzers into a glider. We took some rides in the gliders, which seemed to be made mostly of paper. When towed by an airplane, there was a terrific racket, but once we were cut loose, we floated soundlessly through the air — a beautiful experience.

After graduation, the artillery officers reported to Fort Sill to attend the NDOC. I made a quick trip home and sought to catch up by flying to Oklahoma City. Unfortunately, we could not land in Chicago to change planes because of a heavy fog. I traveled the rest of the way by train and arrived a day late. It had been anticipated that I would incorporate my findings at glider school into the Fort's solution, but I dragged my feet, as I felt foolish. I knew no more about gliders than our students, and they were well aware of the fact. Captain Price, who had done it before, stepped in, but professionally it was a mistake on my part.

Another brother rat, Joe Drewry, arrived at Sill to take the BOC at about this time. Once we went with Clyde to Denton, Texas, to attend a dance at a girls' school. Another time we drove to Fort Worth. Arriving late at night, we could not find a room. We ended up in an underground dive called "The Pirates Den," where we met several cigarette "girls." I say girls because they wore the costumes associated with the trade, but they were twice our age. When the Den closed near dawn, we accompanied them back to their room and talked until several middle-aged men came to pick them up. We napped a little and drove back to the post.

I also made several trips to Dallas to see Evelyn. We usually went to a large barn-like dance hall named The Plantation. As only beer could be sold in Oklahoma, I always brought back a suitcase full of liquor. Once I returned with 17 bottles. There was no taxi at the railroad station, and I had to walk to the bus station. My suitcase was so heavy that I had to put it down every half-block to rest. A cop eyed me suspiciously, but he said nothing.

Most of our spare time, however, was spent near home going to movies, swimming, eating at the Officers Club, and occasionally going to a beer hall in Lawton. Several times I actually went horseback riding. There are few greater thrills than galloping over an open plain. I came to feel a certain fondness for Fort Sill with its vast open spaces that I had never felt for Fort Bragg.

After the airborne outfit passed through, there were no new divisions to be activated for a while. I could finally have the 15-day leave that I had been dreaming of. I arranged to fly from Oklahoma City to Washington, D.C., to save a day. Blair was in Front Royal on her summer vacation, and we renewed our courtship.

I don't remember anything of significance that happened, but when I returned to Fort Sill on a Tuesday, I discovered that the NDOC faculty had been enrolled in the Officers Advanced Course (OAC). As I had been on leave, I was assigned to a class two weeks behind them. Indeed, by arriving on Tuesday I was already two days late and had to do a lot of work to catch up. It was a three-month program formerly called the Field Officers Course. Recently it had been decided to admit qualified officers regardless of rank. I was the only lieutenant, and there were a few captains. The six lieutenant colonels in my section were more typical.

I did not know anybody in my class, but I soon became friends with a Captain Olsen. The weather was miserably hot. The official temperature reached 110°, and in the sun it must have soared to 130°. The barracks was unbelievably hot. Olsen had a car, and we often went to town and bought an ice-cold watermelon, which we ate outside the barracks while waiting, hoping for our rooms to cool down. I continued to go out with Thee and Clyde.

Another brother rat, Jim Cheatham, arrived to take the BOC. He was married, and the Cheatham apartment provided a touch of home where we lonely bachelors gathered. Occasionally, I also went on social outings with Major Hunt, my immediate superior in the NDOC. Near the end of August I bought a 12-cylinder Lincoln coupe from a captain who shared Hunt's quarters. It was a stupid choice, as it was a gas guzzler in a time of gas rationing. With a car, however, my social horizons expanded, and I had accumulated so much stuff that I needed it to move when I got my orders.

It was assumed that we would be pulled out of the Officers Advanced Course when a new division was activated. Therefore, I was not disturbed when I sometimes flunked a test. If I never finished the course, no one would be the wiser. It was too hot to concentrate, and my social activities occupied many evenings. Once Thee went to Dallas with me and had a date with Evelyn's sister, and we had the two girls up to the base.

Then the new division we expected was canceled, and it began to look as though we would finish the course. I began to do enough studying to be sure I passed.

In one exercise I commanded the headquarters battery. I had played infantry regimental commander without a regiment, and critiqued the performance of my superiors acting as battalion commanders, but I had never before commanded a real battery. I knew the ground so well and the school solution so thoroughly that it came off very well.

In early September, I learned that the school had once more tried to get me promoted but that it had been bounced back from Washington. Shortly thereafter, Colonel Draper, who had drafted me to teach at Fort Sill, attended one of our OAC classes and saw that I was still a lieutenant. He went to see Lieutenant Colonel Cox, who had replaced Colonel Smith as the head of the NDOC. The upshot of it was "that they may write a letter asking special consideration in my case. Major Hunt told me this so I would at least have the satisfaction of knowing that I had been recommended." Nothing happened, but around the end of October after I had graduated from OAC 19, I learned that Colonel Pyle, who was high in the school's administration, had told my bosses to recommend me every month and maybe it would slip by. I wrote to my mother with a note attached saying "I am doing a major's work which is probably true as I have been loafing since spring."

In the meantime, nearly all the lieutenants who had been teaching in the various programs of the Field Artillery School for any length of time were notified that they were being made available for reassignments. Clyde, Thee, Macauley, and many others would shortly depart, leaving me bereft of the friends I had been playing with for the past 15 months. I was even omitted from the list of those who were available for reassignment on December 1.

I took advantage of a business trip with Major Hunt to ask him to find out why I was not made available. About ten days later, Colonel Cox called me into his office and asked me what kind of a job I would like when I left Fort Sill. With fond memories of my glider rides, I requested an airborne division. On orders dated November 18, 1943, the headquarters of the Army Ground Forces in Washington relieved me of my duties as of November 30 and assigned me to the 949th Field Artillery Battalion at Fort Bragg. Looking back on it, my haste to depart was a mistake. The school officials may have failed to make me available for reassignment in the hopes they could get me promoted or at least find a good assignment for me. It was a long shot, but the Pentagon sometimes made colossal mistakes. Surely they might accidentally let a lieutenant slip into a captaincy.

I remember very little about my final days at Fort Sill. My last official duty was to prepare a 19-page conference on map reading, which I understand was never used. Hunt took me out to dinner, and in the course of the evening tried to explain why I had been given an excellent rather than a superior efficiency rating. I never saw Thee, Macauley, or him again; and many years were to pass before my path crossed with Clyde's. I am no correspondent, and this episode in my life came to an abrupt end.

I was given seven days' travel time because I went by car, and a weekend was automatically added. I drove night and day to reach home and spend some time with my family. There had been many changes. Elizabeth had married and had made me an uncle a year later. Neville was in Puerto Rico in an engineer battalion undergoing jungle training. Becky had graduated from Hollins, and Ann had taken her place as a student there. That Friday I caught the night train to New York to meet Blair. It was hopelessly late, but we finally got together and went to see Paul Robeson play the lead role in the opera *Othello*. On Sunday we traveled up to Vassar where I spent one night, attended Blair's music class, and took some of her friends to a bar just off campus for a drink.

On my return trip I ran into Sonny Smith, who had become a Marine air force pilot. He took me aside and asked me why I had not been promoted. I had been a first lieutenant for over a year. Promotions in the Army Air Forces and the Marines were rapid, as had been those in the Ground Forces until a few months before. I had no military ambitions, but I had a profound dislike in being thought of as a failure. The basic problem in the Ground Forces was that originally 114 divisions had been planned, but that number had been scaled back to 90. Four were activated in July 1943, and the final two the following month.

The need for the New Division Officers Course had vanished unless there was to be a change of plans. Hence, the instructors had been available for the OAC. The size of officer candidate classes was also drastically curtailed, for there were already 30,000 more officers, for the most part lieutenants, than were needed. Promotions virtually ceased except for the few who held positions requiring higher rank.

Those of us who were extras could either hope to find an authorized
spot in an existing battalion or be shipped overseas as a replacement in a
combat unit. The former was clearly preferable, for it was desirable to
know the men with whom you worked and the standing operating procedures followed by your unit before going into battle.

I reported to the 949th Field Artillery Battalion at Fort Bragg at the
appointed time. It was an old National Guard outfit that had been based in
Detroit and inducted into federal service on April 7, 1941. After spending
over two years at Fort Leonard Wood, Missouri, the battalion had been
sent on maneuvers in the California-Arizona desert for over three months.
The 949th had not reached Fort Bragg until November 1943. It was
undergoing its final training before going overseas when I arrived early
the following month. On paper it was a seasoned outfit, but many of the
best non-commissioned officers had been cadred out or sent to OCS, and
there had been an influx of replacements, mostly from North Carolina.
The difference in accents of these new additions and the Detroiters was so
great that they sometimes had trouble understanding each other, especially on the telephone or radio. The battalion was grossly overstaffed
with officers, for the authorities had decided that it would be better to
place the excess in units where they might get some experience than to
have them twiddling their thumbs in replacement centers.

An infantry division had three organic (*i.e.*, integral) parts of the division: light (105mm howitzers) field artillery battalions and one medium
(155mm howitzers) battalion. When it was heavily engaged in battle,
additional battalions or groups of battalions were attached to give it support. The 949th was a medium battalion that was attached to the 402 Field
Artillery Group while we were at Fort Bragg. The authorized strength of
a battalion was about 29 officers and 500 men. Each battalion consisted of
a headquarters battery, a service battery, and three firing batteries with
four howitzers each. A firing battery had four officers and about 100 men,
commanded by a captain. The executive, a first lieutenant, was in charge
of the howitzers, and he was assisted by a second lieutenant. Finally, there
was another first lieutenant who was designated as the reconnaissance
officer and forward observer.

We had not long been in conflict when I discovered that there were serious disadvantages in being in a separate battalion. When the division we were supporting was pulled out of the line, its artillery got a rest, but the independent battalion was attached to another division and kept on fighting. During the war, we would reinforce the fires of ten different divisions and seven artillery groups. Furthermore, battalions had two-star generals as division commanders and one-star generals as artillery commanders to look after their interests. An independent battalion had only a lieutenant colonel.

A few days after I arrived at Fort Bragg, I informed my mother that I

> was assigned to B Battery, but have no regular job to do as we are over strength. The officers [*in the battalion*] are all Yankees but really know their stuff. The non-commissioned officers are worthless, and 50% of the enlisted men can't read or write. Over half of the battalion are in class V which is the lowest army mental group.

I suppose I got the information from one of the officers who grossly maligned our men. It is true that several were illiterate, and more than once I heard the revealing phrase, "I can read reading, but I can't read writing." Nevertheless, those who served near me were intelligent and conscientious. They were among the finest men I have ever known.

In spite of being over-strength, I was very busy. We had frequent overnight exercises, and one officer in the battery had to be on duty on the weekends. Nevertheless, two thoughts occupied my mind: how to get home for Christmas and how to get a permanent assignment, so that I would no longer be an extra doing odd jobs. The first was resolved more rapidly than I thought possible. I was given a long weekend for Christmas. I set out by car, but it broke down in Hendersonville, and I had to complete the trip by train. Trains were terribly crowded during the war, and I usually had to sit in the aisle on my suitcase, which had caved in under my weight and was shaped like the saddle of a riding horse.

I did get home for a day, saw the family except for Neville, and had a date with Blair. I got off the train at Hendersonville on the way back and found that my car was not fixed. I made two more trips to Hendersonville before I could pick it up near the end of the month.

The military situation was more complex. Our battalion commander was Lieutenant Colonel Russell M. Frink. According to rumor, he had been a vacuum cleaner salesman in civilian life. As one who was not a college graduate, he had an exaggerated idea of the importance of higher education. It was said that nearly every other officer in the battalion had a degree. He must have been impressed by my record — a graduate of V.M.I., an instructor at the Field Artillery School, and a graduate of the Officers Advanced Course. So far as I know, no one in the battalion had attended the last. Instead of seeing in me an over-educated lieutenant devoid of practical experience, he thought I had something special to offer.

Around the middle of January, Colonel McMahon, the group commander, summoned me to his office. He left me standing at attention while he spent some minutes grilling me on my qualifications. He especially wanted to know why I had not been a cadet officer at V.M.I. When he dismissed me, he told me that he would let me know what he had for me that afternoon. I never heard from him. He always wore his riding pants and boots, which made me wonder if he was not a product of the past. I suspect he told Frink that I should get some experience as a regular battery officer, because the next day I was appointed the reconnaissance officer of Battery B after the previous holder of that position was transferred to battalion headquarters. At last I had found a home.

Edward C. Seddon, the battery commander, was a short, soft-spoken, cultured man about my age who was to become a highly successful lawyer and businessman after the war. He had an attractive wife who had accompanied him to the post. The other two officers were bachelors. Herbert W. Strecker, a big, roughly hewn but kindly man, was the executive, and William J. Hawks was the assistant executive.

As reconnaissance officer, I was in charge of training the communication, survey, and instrument personnel. In war I would man an observation post or go as a forward observer with the infantry. I immediately set about training my men, as we were to undergo the Army Ground Forces test in February to see if we were ready to go overseas. Few of our enlisted men had ever been to high school, but they were willing students. As far as I was concerned, I had the best job in the battery.

The Army Ground Forces tests went off very well. I was sent forward to an observation post and given a target. I had studied the terrain and quickly began to fire. The first volley was just over the target. I came down 200 yards, got a short, and went into fire for effect on the third volley. The acceptable solution was to get within 400 yards of the target on the first volley. I had beat the school solution by one volley and some precious seconds. The umpire gave me a score of 95. One reason for my success was that the battalion had a terrain board where artillery observers could practice. Our officers' classes, which were usually held four nights a week, frequently concentrated on adjusting fire. I also used the board in the daytime and trained my men to use forward observer methods.

About this time, an officer in group headquarters told me that Colonel McMahon was going to do something for me. A little later, Colonel Frink called me into his office and began to tell me of a position that had been found for me. Obviously hurt and without waiting for him to finish, I said I would rather stay where I was. I had found a job I liked and could do well. I had no desire to change. He agreed to keep me. On looking back, I regret my haste. I would like to have known what the new position was. More importantly, Frink and perhaps others had gone to considerable trouble to find a captain's job for me. I should have thanked him profusely.

Another time when I was in Colonel Frink's office, he lectured me on leadership. Few people, he said, could be leaders, but anybody could be a driver. His goal was to make me more dynamic, but I immediately saw that he was describing himself. I doubt if a single man in the battalion really liked him, but no one would deny that he knew his job thoroughly. His never-ending drive transformed the 500 officers and men he commanded into an excellent battalion. We obeyed in part from fear and in part because we knew that to succeed we had to follow his orders.

Colonel Frink had no hesitation in cussing out his officers in front of their men. Once before dawn when a very capable lieutenant made a mistake while leading the entire battalion in exercises, the Colonel bellowed at him, calling him a fool and telling him what command to give. Few of

us had escaped a tongue-lashing at one time or another. His actions drove
the officers and enlisted men into an unconscious alliance against him.
Still, and here he was right, his very drive carried the day.

On April 8, the officers of the battalion had a party. Someone got Harry
November and me blind dates. A battalion survey officer, Harry, or
"Crash" as we called him, had a first-rate mind and was to prove to be a
brave and able soldier. But he had a unique capacity to always say or do
the wrong thing as far as military protocol went — hence, his nickname
Crash. We picked up our dates in Fayetteville and took in the officers club
as well as the party. My date was pretty, and I began to take her out on
Wednesdays, our night off.

I got home for a brief visit, the final one before going overseas. Blair
was there, having graduated from Vassar a month or two early because of
the wartime speed-up. The only thing I remember is that my mother had
tears in her eyes when I departed. It was one of the only two times I ever
saw her almost cry. There must have been other events as well.

In a letter home on April 30, I responded to one I had received: "So my
exit caused quite a comment. Can't see why everyone should think that
Blair and I are secretly engaged." We had talked of marriage for a year or
two, but Blair wanted to finish college. Now that she was through, my
imminent departure for Europe made it impractical. In that same letter, I
reported that our battalion had loaded its stuff onto a train, but for some
reason had been told to take it off. Two of our battalions in the 402 Field
Artillery Group were already in England.

Because of the delay, Blair decided to visit me. Her mother arranged for
her to stay with friends, Colonel Underwood and his wife, who lived on
the post. She arrived during the afternoon of May 7. I had sold my car to
Lieutenant Heilman, one of the officers in the battery. Happily for me, he
was restricted to the post for some heinous crime and kindly let me use it.

During her visit, I had to spend one night in a foxhole and another on
duty, but we did have five evenings together. We "went to a movie and to
town to dance twice. The rest of the evenings we just sat and talked."

The Underwoods were most kind to us. Because they had had to pick up Blair and put her on the train when I was tied up during the day, I asked father to send them a case of preserves or jelly.

About this time I had a blow. My chief of detail, Sergeant Burman, had to be released because he had tuberculosis. His departure left me with two corporals and a number of privates. John W. Currie was promoted to take his place and held the job until the end of the war. Since we had turned in nearly all our equipment, the authorities had a problem keeping us busy.

In late May the battalion took a practice march to Wrightsville Beach. I loaned my men $25 so they could buy bathing suits and basked in the sun all day with a light heart. The Fort Bragg sun had not affected me, but I had underestimated that of the Atlantic. I got the worst sunburn in my life. I still remember painfully submitting to Strecker's touch as he applied lotion to my back.

On our return to Bragg, I was appointed trial judge advocate in a court-martial case. The accused had been absent without leave. To win a conviction, all I had to do was to present the company book, which listed him as absent. I had a 100-percent record of success as a lawyer, but every time I submitted the written record of this case, it bounced because of some technicality or a misspelled word.

The waiting was getting on everyone's nerves. On June 5, I told my mother that I missed "my car and Blair's company a lot. . . . Both are pretty essential in this hole." Blair must have been equally bored in Front Royal.

On June 12, I was summoned to answer a long-distance telephone call in battalion headquarters. Blair had decided we should marry immediately and had taken her mother to Riverside three days before to inform my parents. There were a number of men in headquarters, and I had to tell her somehow that we had finally received our orders and were about to depart, all without being specific, because our move was classified Secret. On June 13, our battalion entrained for Camp Shanks, a post on the Hudson River a few miles north of the New York City suburbs.

At Shanks we made our final preparation for embarkation. I ran into

Colonel Smith, my NDOC commander. He was surprised to see that I was still a lieutenant, for at the time he had left Fort Sill, the school's recommendations for promotion had been automatically approved.

The only other event that I remember was when the battalion was lined up shirtless and marched single file between rows of medics who inoculated us against every disease known to man. One soldier fainted, but the rest of us survived being stuck first in one arm and then the other.

Our ship was not ready, so we were permitted to go into New York City for a day. Instead, I wrote letters to thank the Underwoods and to make my peace with Blair and my parents. To the latter, I had to explain why I had not informed them of my intention to marry.

> [I] really don't see why you were so surprised. In fact I thought you expected it. I was willing when I got through V.M.I., but Blair wanted to finish school and figured she was a little young. When she finished at Vassar, she was willing, but I wasn't as I expected to go overseas soon. However she suggested it in several letters and at last I agreed as it began to look like we would never leave. You see definite plans did not develop until the last minute. . . . Sure hated to call it off and hope I didn't hurt Blair's feelings.

Then I made a noble gesture. I did not want to be tied down myself, but I knew that my chances would be few while hers would be many.

> Incidently [*sic*], we aren't engaged, so there is no reason at all for her to sit around and not have dates. The primary reason why I was so secretive was that I knew you all would look askance at everything she did and every time she went out with a boy. Just brought this up so you all wouldn't think she was two-timing me when she went out.
>
> Thanks a lot for your efforts for the wedding and am sorry it was necessary to disappoint Father. Sure wish I could have married her.

Somehow my letters restored peace and understanding, but they did not alter the basic situation. For the next year, Blair was to put her training as a bacteriologist into practice as a supervisor of a laboratory that produced penicillin at the Hayden Chemical Corporation at Princeton Junction, New Jersey, and I was to fight in the war in Europe.

On June 20, 1944, the battalion sailed down the Hudson on a ferry boat and boarded the *Queen Elizabeth*, which was in use as a troopship. Two weeks before, on June 6 — D-Day — the first wave of our invading forces had landed in Normandy. We were finally going to join our comrades in arms.

Chapter 4

The "Phantom" War

OUR 949TH FIELD ARTILLERY BATTALION was assigned to act as the Military Police (MP) aboard the *Queen Elizabeth*. It meant loss of sleep because of guard duty, but there were two advantages: it gave us something to do, and we had the run of the ship. With my MP arm badge, I could go from the top of the ship, where the nurses sunbathed, down to the lowest deck. There were about 16,000 people aboard, and the crowded conditions could have provoked strife. The only difficulty we encountered occurred when a drunken lieutenant tried to force his way into the nurses' quarters but was forcibly halted by one of our corporals. We put him under arrest, and Colonel Frink assured me that he would be prosecuted. The senior officer in charge of replacements intervened on the lieutenant's behalf. I have a feeling that everyone was too busy to worry about his hitting a guard, and in the end he got off free.

Our men were quartered in a large, windowless room that in peacetime had been used to store baggage. We officers fared much better; 14 of us shared a stateroom. Four levels of bunks were attached to the wall except under the porthole, where there were only three. There was barely room to squeeze in underneath the bunk above you. We had a bath, but only salt water was available as the storage for fresh water had been designed for the normal number of passengers on a cruise.

We ate in shifts, and only two meals were served each day. They were first-rate, however. Breakfast consisted of fruit, cereal, and fish before the bacon and eggs. Soup and fish courses preceded dinner and dessert. We had a Cockney waiter who kept us amused, but after we gave him a handsome tip near the end of the voyage, he disappeared from sight. During the whole trip, the only amusement we had was an afternoon tea dance provided by Glenn Miller's orchestra. The band leader had gone on ahead, but his musicians were kept busy playing for the officers and men.

Our unescorted ship zigzagged across the Atlantic Ocean. In theory, we should have been able to outrun any enemy submarine. I am sure that would have been true if the sub was behind us, but what if it was in front? An antiaircraft battalion had been assigned to man the guns, but they had never fired them. There may have been enough lifeboats for the few women aboard, but if we had been hit, it would have been a long swim for most of us. The authorities apparently knew what they were doing, however. The *Queen Elizabeth* encountered no difficulty on its numerous crossings. I had never been at sea and occasionally felt slightly sick; but on the whole, it was a pleasant voyage.

We arrived at Greenock, Scotland, on June 28, 1944, and entrained for Leominister, Herefordshire, in England. It was dusk when we passed through Carlisle, where the train stopped long enough for the Red Cross to feed us coffee and doughnuts. After that, all was dark until we arrived at our destination. We were quartered in a tent camp in Berrington Park, about three miles north of the town. Except for showers and toilet facilities, the camp was primitive.

My tent was within 200 yards of a late-18th-century hall. One evening, several other officers and I visited the grounds and met an old gentleman, who turned out to be Lord Crawley, the owner. We helped him pick several quarts of strawberries, and he and his wife treated us to some of the fruit — figs, dates, and gooseberries. The Crawleys took us on a tour of their home filled with many treasures. The property now belongs to the National Trust, thanks to the heavy estate taxes assessed after the war.

Leominister was a town of about 7,000 inhabitants, and noted for an old, but much remodeled, church and more to the point, a late-18th-century pub. I had a blind date with an American nurse from a nearby hospital. With some other couples, we headed for this most venerable of English institutions. Alcoholic beverages were rationed. We started with scotch and ginger. After it was gone, we turned to gin and lemon, then to beer, and finally to hard cider. The English must have hated us for cluttering up their pubs and consuming all the daily ration. The pub closed a little after ten, and we sojourned to the hospital where we played ping pong in the nurses' recreation room.

Two days later, I returned to the pub and ran into some officers who were recovering from wounds received in the Normandy invasion. One was a tank platoon commander who regaled us with stories about how he and General J. Lawton "Lightning Joe" Collins, the commander of the VII Corps, had ensured the success of the D-Day landing and the expansion of the bridgehead. As this lieutenant told it, he and the General were in daily contact and continually saved the day. We took his stories with a grain of salt, but I do remember his warning: avoid the 90th Infantry Division, known as the poorest in the U.S. Army and the only one that had disgraced itself.

The American authorities made every effort to prevent friction between our troops and the British. There were frequent complaints that the Americans were "over-paid, over-sexed, and over here." Nothing could be done about the last two, but the first could be reduced by persuading troops to put most of their pay in government bonds or other investments. I reduced my pay to $25 a month, bought war bonds, and was duly thankful when it came time to buy a house for my rapidly growing family in 1954. We were also informed that "bloody" was a terrible cuss word that we must never say in front of the English. "Bloody" immediately became a part of every oath. If our men learned nothing else during their stay in England, it was this one word — a word they would never have thought of using if it had not been forbidden.

While we were waiting for orders, I found time to visit the Ludlow Castle ruins, steeped in history, about eight miles north of our camp. Here King Henry VIII's older brother, Arthur, had spent his last days with his bride, Catherine of Aragon. I also went into Worcester for an evening date with an English girl.

It was a welcome change when our battery was sent to a 40-room mansion near Stratford-Upon-Avon, the birthplace of William Shakespeare, to prepare a camp for an incoming unit. For a brief time I had a private room and bath. I had one day off and visited Warwick Castle and the sights in Stratford. In the evening I took in Shakespeare's play, *A Midsummer Night's Dream*, at the Royal Shakespeare Theatre.

Most of my time was spent training my men. By July 13, we had drawn our combat equipment and moved to the village of Ogborne St. George in Wiltshire, where we were housed in a brick barracks. We went out on a firing range near the town of Salisbury to try out our howitzers. During our march, we caught a glimpse of the 13th-century Gothic Salisbury Cathedral and passed within two miles of the prehistoric monument Stonehenge.

Once I was sent to a warehouse to requisition some clothing. I intended to check each item, but the sergeants there insisted that they would do it and that I would be in the way, so I wandered around town. When I returned, they loaded nicely packed boxes in the truck, and I signed for them. Upon my return to the battalion, our Supply sergeants found that the boxes contained various leftover articles of clothing that bore little relation to what I was supposed to have. From this, I learned never to trust anyone in Supply. Someone must have covered for me, because I heard no more about it. I hope our Supply people found a competent envoy and got what they needed on future requisitions. In any case, I was never sent on a Supply mission again.

While quartered in Ogborne, I went to a movie in nearby Swindon and found a shop in another small town, Marlborough, where bottles of scotch could be purchased. I was also sent somewhere to take a two-hour course and ran into four officers who had been in my OAC class. To top that, two more appeared who had been in glider school with me. One of them introduced me to another Lieutenant Major. It turned out that we had a common 18th-century ancestor. His line had moved to Kentucky and then to Missouri, while mine had stayed in Virginia. We both had been incorrectly taught that the family seat was Hursley, not 20 miles from where we were standing. I was delighted to report the encounter to my father, who was interested in genealogy.

On August 3, 1944, the battalion moved to the assembly area on the outskirts of Southampton. I was to look back fondly on that night, for I slept in a warm bed for one last night in England. There was also plenty to eat, and coffee was always available in the wardroom. The following day, we were loaded into five landing craft vehicles with all our equipment, and just after midnight we set sail for Normandy.

On the morning of August 5, we ran ashore on Utah Beach during high tide. The wreckage of every sort of combat vehicle still cluttered the beach, but the dead had long before been removed. In the afternoon after the tide had gone out, the mouths of our landing crafts opened and our jeeps, tracks, and howitzers rolled off onto the sand. Within 30 minutes, the entire battalion was ashore in France.

We passed through Ste-Mère-Eglise, a little town in total ruins, on our way to a bivouac area among the hedgerows. We gained firsthand knowledge of why it had taken so long for U.S. forces to break out of the Cotentin Peninsula. Each tiny field was enclosed by a tall hedge on either side of a sunken road only wide enough to permit a wagon to pass along. The sunken lanes provided ideal trenches for the defenders. If one was captured, there was another one 50 or so yards away. It is hard to imagine worse terrain for tanks.

On August 6, I wrote my parents. Most of my letter was devoted to asking them to do errands for me, such as collecting for my car which I had sold on time, buying war bonds, and the like. Indeed, nearly all my letters were full of requests. My parents must have felt part of the war effort. In view of censorship, all I could write about my own activities after spending 24 hours in Normandy was, "Have no news at all to write about."

We had arrived at an opportune moment. The initial landing on Utah Beach, on June 6, had been very successful, but our troops had been brought to a halt when they reached the hedgerows. The British landing had not been costly either, but Field Marshal Bernard Montgomery had failed to take Caen on the first day as projected. With the Supreme Allied Commander General Dwight D. Eisenhower, Montgomery had played a principal role in planning OPERATION OVERLORD and had been commander of all the ground troops, including the Americans, up until D-Day. (After Montgomery went ashore at Normandy, the command was split.) Nevertheless, over a month elapsed before he took Caen, which had been his first day's objective.

To the east of Caen lay the shortest route to Paris, and there were no hedgerows to impede progress. For this reason, the Germans had concentrated considerable forces in Montgomery's sector to prevent an Allied breakthrough of their lines. His inaction made it necessary for the Americans to battle through the hedgerows to his west.

At first, progress had been dishearteningly slow, but near the end of July, General Omar N. Bradley launched a mighty assault that achieved a breakthrough. By the time we landed, the Third Army had been activated and a fluid situation had developed. The town of Avranches, near the Normandy-Brittany border, had been captured, and our troops were spreading out to the west in Brittany, to the south toward the Loire River, and to the east toward the Seine River and Paris.

On August 7, we moved through St. Lo, Coutances, and Avranches. As we approached the last named city, we heard the distant rumble of artillery. The Germans were counterattacking in the Mortain area about 20 miles away. For the first time, we heard the guns of war.

When elements of the Third Army reached Le Mans, they swung to the north to try to join Montgomery's army group and thereby encircle the two German armies that had been defending Normandy. The 949th was given the mission of supporting the 80th Infantry Division of the XX Corps in its drive to take Sillé-le-Guillaume on the left flank of the main effort.

We occupied our positions at dawn on August 10, after traveling most of the night, and I was given my first mission as a forward observer. All I remember is leaving my jeep and driver at the foot of a hill and running up to the top with a couple of my men. There was some sniper fire near us, but we had no close shaves. Private C, my driver, became so frightened that I never used him again. Other than that, no lessons were learned and we accomplished nothing. During the course of the day I was recalled, and our battalion moved off to the east.

The decision to move to the east cost me whatever chance there was to be among the forward observers who directed fire on the Germans on their push through the Falaise Gap. I have always heard that they had a field day, with continuous targets of men, horses, tanks, and other vehicles.

The Normandy breakthrough was hailed as a great Allied victory. Only recently, as I read the history of the campaign, did I learn that it was also a failure of Allied leadership. General George S. Patton had urged the drive to the north to cut off the German retreat, but the cautious Bradley had actually ordered him to halt before the gap was closed. Montgomery had moved to the south with his usual slowness, and General Eisenhower, the overall commander, did nothing to correct the situation. The Falaise Gap was never closed. About 270,000 Germans were in the pocket and another 50,000 were west of the Seine River. The Allies killed, wounded, or captured about 80,000 German soldiers. Some 240,000 men, 28,000 vehicles, and several hundred tanks escaped to form a line from the North Sea to the Swiss border.

General Patton urged another envelopment with the Third Army sweeping down the Seine to catch the Germans who escaped the Falaise Gap and the other troops west of the river. He also advocated a grand sweep north of Paris through Beauvais, but the senior Allied commanders gave him little heed. They were content with their partial success and dreamed of an early German capitulation. The Germans, on the other hand, could hardly believe their good fortune to have escaped to fight again.

Our battalion moved slowly in the direction of the Seine River and went into position to the east and a little to the south of Chartres on August 16. I was part of the reconnaissance party that was sent on ahead to choose our exact position. The famed 13th-century Gothic cathedral soared high above the treeless plain, but few of the other buildings in the city could be seen. I will always remember crying, "aiming point, that cathedral" as I brought our four howitzers into position. Whenever I tell this story, lovers of art cringe in horror. Actually, an aiming point is used to point the howitzers in the same direction as the target. We then moved the barrels of the howitzers to the right or to the left a prescribed number of degrees before we fired. No artillery rounds fell in the heart of the city.

Our mission was to support the 7th Armored Division. On the previous evening, August 15, part of one of its combat teams had entered Chartres from the northwest, and simultaneously another part had entered from the southwest to sweep the city clean. According to gossip, one of the columns took the wrong street and in the twilight shot it out with the other, while the Germans watched from the windows. The official history makes no mention of this episode and is content to say that the columns met determined opposition. No wonder, if they met each other. The brigadier general who commanded the combat team was relieved a few weeks later.

Since there were no troops between us and the city, Sergeant Carroll, our Supply sergeant, took a few men and dug foxholes about 25 yards in front of our position. Perhaps some Germans were sent out to cause us trouble, but our greatest danger came from Supply elements of the 7th Armored, who were on our right flank. The trigger-happy rascals insisted on firing their machine guns all across the front and didn't miss Carroll's men by much. The next day, our first fire missions bombed the approaches of the city to aid the 7th Armored, but again the Germans held on. Finally, someone had the wisdom to see that tanks were not the best weapons to capture the ancient city with narrow, winding streets. The 7th Armored was dispatched to the east, and the 5th Infantry Division was given the mission of mopping up the Germans in the city.

I was sent to join one of the 7th Armored Division battalions as a forward observer. By sheer chance I was assigned to ride in the tank of my V.M.I. brother rat, Gordon Moore. He was frankly horrified at the thought of having someone like me who had never been in a tank replace a man he needed. I was equally upset at the prospect and could not see how I could accomplish anything. There was no room for my 90-pound radio that I used to call for artillery fire. While we were facing this dilemma, the weather-beaten battalion commander summoned his officers to a conference. He castigated them for taking prisoners a day or two before, and told them they were to stop being so "chicken" in the future. I was shocked. It is certainly true that prisoners slow down armored operations, but I had read so many books about gallant soldiers who always obeyed the laws of war that I was dumbfounded. There were no tears shed on my part when I heard a rumor several weeks later that the battalion commander had been killed.

I would like to be able to report that someone in higher authority had the wisdom to discover that an artillery observer in a tank without means to communicate with his battalion was useless baggage and only got in the way. I cannot do so. The 949th's mission was changed to support the 5th Infantry Division, and I was recalled right after hearing the battalion commander's lecture. I did not see Gordon again until our 50th V.M.I. class reunion.

The 7th Armored Division had had very little combat experience when we were briefly together; but as was so often the case, once a few rough edges were straightened out, it became a splendid outfit as proven by its gallant defense of St. Vith during the Battle of the Bulge, December 1944.

The 5th Infantry was an experienced division of an unusually high caliber. We gave it support from August 18 until early September, when we were halted a little beyond the Meuse River for lack of gas for our vehicles. I should say we followed in the 5th's wake as best we could. I do not believe that we had fired a single round during the entire period.

From Chartres, our route took us through Fontainebleau, Provins, Epernay, Reims, and the Argonne Forest, to the vicinity of the village of Vacherauville, Meuse. The press wrote eloquently of our rapid advance, but to those of us who participated, it was a period of discomfiture and boredom.

France can be miserably hot in August. We were clad in wool uniforms, and in Patton's Army we wore buttoned collars with neatly tied neckties. There were no roofs on the jeeps, and the windshields rested on the hood because they reflected light in upright positions, drawing gunfire. As a result, our faces became badly sunburned, and to the sweat and sunburn was added a thick layer of dirt. We spent much of our time on unpaved side roads, and dust was constantly blowing in our faces.

A second problem was that we were rarely issued anything but K rations to eat. A day's K ration consisted of three rectangular boxes, each containing a small can of meat or cheese and a few crackers. It kept you alive but provided no culinary delight. Finally, there was the boredom. A 40-mile advance that electrified the press meant that we were moving at a rate of about three miles an hour when we were awake. Sometimes our vehicles were parked on the road; sometimes we moved at a rate of 10 or 15 miles an hour; sometimes we crept forward and I got out and walked beside my jeep

Writing letters home helped fill the time. On August 17, I wrote my

mother that "Life here isn't so bad except that we are generally tired and always dirty." By the 26th, I was more vehement and sent forth an appeal for cookies and cocoa that could be mixed with water: "Am sick and tired of this K ration. It consists of about two mouthfuls of concentrated calories. It sustains life ok, but I always ate for pleasure not to live." We sought to supplement our diet by trading cigarettes for eggs.

At this point, I had been in France for three weeks and reported that I "have already washed and changed my clothes three times." This was accomplished by stripping off my clothes, filling my helmet with water, and sponging off as best I could. Once when I was so engaged, two teenage French girls wandered through our camp. My condition did not seem to bother them, but I lacked their sangfroid.

My brother Neville was looking forward to being sent overseas. I could only advise that "he is due for a disappointment. He will always be tired, dirty, and hungry, . . . but worst of all bored to death." Two days later I received a cable from Neville saying he was about to get married. After sending my congratulations on the 28th of August, I remarked that this will be "the third wedding I have missed since the war — Eliz's, yours, and my own." Then on a different subject:

> Hear you may take a voyage soon. A tip from an old soldier to a rookie — take a good bath and change your clothes within a week before sailing as you may not get a chance after that. It is just like maneuvers over here. We make a reconnaissance all day, march all night and go into position at dawn only to find the Germans out of range again.

There were, of course, periods of exuberance. When we went through towns in Normandy, the inhabitants rushed out and filled our canteen cups with cognac, wine, or cider. I described our reception in a letter home:

> Their cognac is close to 200 proof. A glass would knock out anyone, so after a trip of about 30 miles, one is generally pretty happy. They yell "good day" at us as we go by, and we reply with a "bonjour." I like the French a lot.

To the east of Chartres, we stumbled upon a French woman who invited us into her house. The Germans had departed a few hours before, and we celebrated with her daughter by drinking her cognac and some gin we happened to have. She had a jewelry store in a nearby town and before our departure gave us a good luck charm and a fleur de lis. I bought a ring for 1,300 francs in return, which insured her a handsome profit from our visit as I doubt if it was worth a dime.

On the outskirts of Fontainebleau, we drove past an elementary school. The children and their teachers were standing by the road waving French and American flags and singing the French anthem, "Marseillaises." We didn't know where we were going, but we yelled "à Paris!" It seemed to please them.

I was sent forward on a mission and crossed the Seine on a bridge the engineers had built. Before I had gone far, I was recalled as the situation was changing so fast. Our battery's position was in the beautiful Fontainebleau forest. A Frenchman gave Ed Seddon, our battery commander, a bottle of champagne, which we enjoyed. We thought every Frenchman had a cellar full. It was only when I returned to France seven years after the war that I learned that many of them had saved their last bottles to celebrate on the liberation day and had generously shared them with us.

Our greatest experience of French generosity came when we liberated the province of Champagne. We passed through Epernay in the morning with our canteen cups extended. I felt a warm glow by the time we emerged on the far side of the city and struck out for Reims some 15 miles away. We arrived in the early afternoon. The bridge over the Aisne River had been destroyed, and it was necessary to crisscross back and forth through the city. The pressing crowds brought our column to long halts, girls swarmed over our vehicles and were generous with their kisses, although how they could bear to get near such dirty men I do not know. Our canteen cups were filled as fast as we could empty them. I saw one large American airman in civilian clothes with his arm around a pretty girl. He had been shot down, and the French had hidden him until our arrival.

By the time we reached the open plains on the other side of the city, dusk was approaching. A German plane strafed us unsuccessfully, but in our inebriated state we waved merrily at the pilot. It seemed to us that rarely did planes hit anything in this type of situation. Indeed, it seemed that the speed was so great that a bullet hit the ground only about every 50 feet, or more.

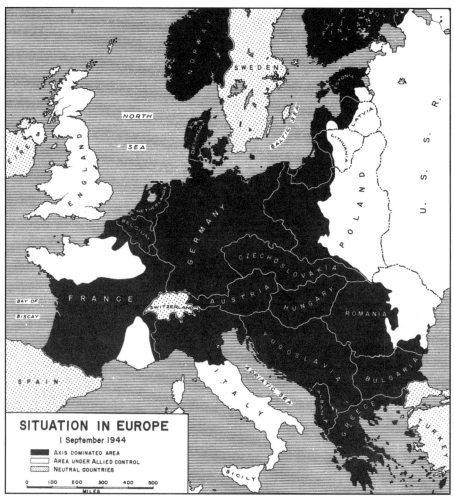

SITUATION IN EUROPE
I September 1944

▪ AXIS DOMINATED AREA
☐ AREA UNDER ALLIED CONTROL
▨ NEUTRAL COUNTRIES

0   100   200   300   400   500
MILES

From *United States Army in World War II: The European Theater of Operations — The Lorraine Campaign*, by Hugh M. Cole (Washington, D.C.: Historical Division, Dept. of Army, 1950), 7.

Near Verdun in early September, Captain Don Kilbourn, our Battalion S-2, told me that our next objective was Frankfurt, and we hoped to get there in a couple of weeks. If we had, the war would have been virtually over, because we would have had a substantial bridgehead over the Rhine River, with no further natural barriers to prevent us from spreading over most of Germany. Unhappily, shortly after receiving this news, we again ran out of gas. Not totally out as the newsreel broadcasters would have one believe, but tactically out. We always had enough to maneuver a little in case there was a battle.

The week we were halted had tragic consequences. The Germans were only beginning to pour troops into the forts just west of Metz and into a line to protect the Moselle River. The ground was still hard, and the rivers were still in their banks. There is no doubt that we could have easily taken Metz if we had had the gas. Whether we could have crossed the Saar and Rhine rivers cannot be said, but we could certainly have gotten into a position to try, and I think we would have succeeded. Instead of giving what gas there was to Patton's fast-moving troops, it went to the cautious Montgomery's force.

There were some compensations for the delay. Our mail began to catch up with us. I had heard almost nothing from my mother and Blair since landing in Normandy, except for a cable from the latter. Now I began to get letters from her two or three times a week and once a week from my mother. Real food began to reach us, a welcome change from K rations. Once we were on the move again, those three rectangular boxes became our staple diet, augmented when possible by eggs and chicken bartered from the French.

More ominous was that the rains began. September through November are the rainy months in Lorraine, and in 1944 there was nearly three times as much as usual. It was not a hard rain, but rather an almost continuous drizzle. The weather also began to turn cold. I knew enough history to be aware that civilized armies went into winter quarters when it got cold, and I wondered if we would. Had I known the answer, I would have really been discouraged.

On September 7, we were on the move again. Our battalion was assigned to support the 90th Infantry Division. We had heard bad rumors about their performance in Normandy, which made us not too happy. Our worries were unfounded. A new division commander and a little experience had made it one of the finest divisions in Europe, which provides proof that the commander of a unit, whether large or small, is the determining factor of how it performs.

I was sent as a forward observer to the first battalion of the 358th Infantry Regiment. My team consisted of a radio operator from the Midwest named Ray Speaker and a scout corporal from North Carolina named Burton D. Isenhour. We had trained together at Fort Bragg, and they had been with me on my uneventful missions in France. They were brave men who knew their jobs thoroughly and possessed important traits that I lacked. I have absolutely no sense of direction. They did. Try as I would, I could not escape lapsing into daydreams. They were constantly on the alert and most observant. My contribution lay in map reading, which I had taught at Fort Sill, and in adjusting fire. We were a congenial threesome, and I became devoted to them.

We spent the night in a schoolhouse that served as the first battalion headquarters, and Captain Gene White, our liaison officer, was there. That night the 106th Panzer Brigade launched a counterattack designed to slow the American advance. The Germans slipped between two infantry regiments and stumbled onto the command post of the 90th Division, which was well to the rear. The division headquarters and staff scattered, and according to gossip, General "Wild Bill" Weaver took to the woods in his pajamas. Actually, he was in his droopy underwear, which he came close to losing as he organized the defense. Happily, the Germans failed to realize the importance of their find. The command post must have contained information concerning our plans and the disposition of our forces. Instead of searching for documents, the Germans split up into three or four columns and began to return to their own lines. The 90th moved quickly to block their escape.

The company to which I was attached was sent west to the village of Mairy to block a possible escape route. Our artillery battalion was so far to the rear that we could not reach it from the town by radio. We drove several hundred yards uphill on a road to the south of the village in the hope of establishing communication. As I was standing beside our jeep, an infantry lieutenant told me that a German armored column was approaching. I ran up to the top of the hill. Sure enough, a number of tanks and armored vehicles were approaching Mairy down a sunken road beside a creek some 200 yards away. I had no difficulty identifying them as German as there were flanges on the muzzles of their guns while we had none. By then, Speaker had found that he could reach our liaison plane, and the pilot could relay our commands to the battery. We went into action.

Speaker was sheltered by the cut in the hill made for the road. My plan

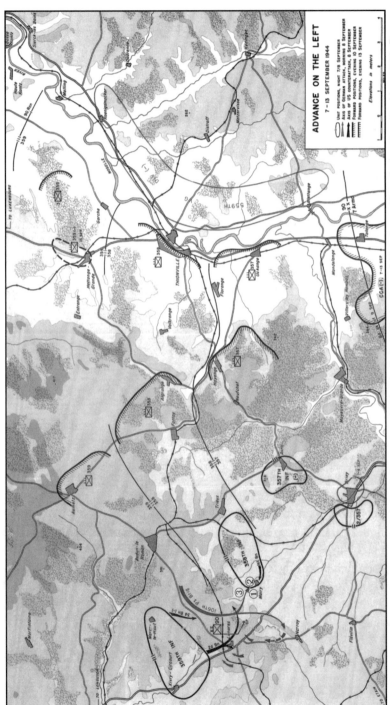

The American Army's advance on its left, 7-13 September 1944. #1, 2, 3, indicate Russell Major's positions facing the attacking 106th Panzer Brigade. (From *United States Army in World War II: The European Theater of Operations — The Lorraine Campaign*, by Hugh M. Cole (Washington, D.C.: Historcal Division, Dept. of the Army, 1950), Map XV.

was to leave him there and to adjust fire from the crest of the hill, keeping Isenhour in a sheltered position half-way between us to relay my commands. Ike, as we often called him, had no intention of missing the fun. He crouched a few yards from me on top of the hill. As it turned out, Speaker could hear me above the noise of battle. I called for fire. It was a tricky situation. Our battery was far to the west, and the enemy was between me and my guns. This meant that I had to do everything in reverse. Otherwise, it was a forward observer's dream.

The lead German tank was knocked out by the infantry. Those immediately to the rear could not turn around because of the narrow sunken road. Farther back, the creek prevented maneuvering to their left. There was utter confusion as shell after shell fell among them. I noted that time and again a man would jump out of a tank or armored car and attempt to carry a message to another vehicle. Almost invariably, he was quickly killed. Only recently did I learn that few German tanks were equipped with radios. The German commander was probably in one of the lead tanks. Stalled as he was on a sunken road, he had no way to direct his troops in the rear who were still in a position to maneuver. The column did pull off to the side of the road on a hillside, but without direction no effort was made to attack the village from another angle.

Once, one of the tanks spotted me and fired a shell that hit several yards in front of me, but luckily the fragments flew to either side. I ducked down and came up about 20 yards from where I had been and continued to order fire. In my haste I had left Isenhour at the top, but he quickly joined me. Actually there was no need for him to be in an exposed position, but he was determined to miss nothing.

Captain White interrupted us several times by radio pointing out that we were firing behind our own lines. Did we have permission? The answer was no, but happily no one stopped us. White's concern was justified. About this time, the infantry lieutenant who had told me about the tanks arrived and pointed out that several Germans were on the far side of Mairy. This suggested that the village had been taken, and he asked me to fire on it. I gave the necessary commands, but before the first salvo, I noticed several Americans standing in the street. I halted fire just in time. What was to be my finest hour almost became a terrible tragedy.

The battle had begun a little before 8:50 a.m., and it was over by 10. Officially, we fired 331 rounds, but I was told after the battle that the figure was over 400. The 949th Field Artillery Battalion's operational narrative listed 5 tiger tanks and 20 armored vehicles destroyed. I never counted them, but I didn't see any escape. German records reveal that only 9 tanks and assault guns and one-fourth of the men in the 106th Panzer Brigade found their way back to their lines.

I wandered down into the village when the battle was over and heard one infantryman tell another, "That lieutenant sure can shoot." The other replied that the shells came too close. He was right, and he didn't know how close they would have come if I had not halted fire on the village just in time. Actually, I never asked for fire closer than a hundred yards from the village, but even if no one made a mistake, the normal dispersion might cause a shell to fall 50 yards long or short.

Isenhour, Speaker, and I wandered over the battlefield. I had seen very few direct hits, but most of the vehicles were out of range of the infantry's bazookas and other weapons. Either Isenhour or Speaker crawled into one tank and found the Germans dead. There was no sign of blood or evidence that anything had penetrated the tank, but there were three or four shell holes no more than a yard away. I suppose the concussion killed them.

The picture that remains most firmly in my mind is of a blond, blue-eyed soldier about my age whose chest was pretty well blown off. Photographs he had been carrying were scattered around him. Several were plainly of his mother and probably sisters; others were of a pretty girl — his wife or betrothed, I do not know. I carried several photographs of Blair, which I occasionally looked at longingly when I was alone. My elation at our victory rapidly dissolved.

My spirits had recovered by the time I wrote my mother on September 11:

> Am generally bored to death and so spend most of my time sleeping, however, a battle is quite exciting — just like riding on a roller coaster. The horrors of war are greatly exaggerated so don't worry.

I continued to trail along with the 358th Infantry as it fought its way into Thionville several days after I wrote the above letter. This important town was sprawled out on either side of the Moselle River. I occupied an

Observation Post on high ground overlooking the town. Someone else had another OP not too far away. We were to measure the angle to every artillery flash to determine the location of the enemy battery. Counter-battery fire was to follow once this had been done. It was all in preparation for an infantry crossing. I stayed up the entire night, but nothing happened. Around eight in the morning, I learned that the attack had been called off, and we were to follow the 90th Division to the south toward Metz. The authorities had forgotten to tell us, and we had lost a good night's sleep.

My next OP was on a wooded hill overlooking Maizières-les-Metz. An observer of the 7th Armored Division had occupied the spot before me. Whether he found any targets, I do not know, but he did uncover a buried jug that must have held at least ten gallons of wine. He left nothing for his relief, and we were unsuccessful in our search for another bottle. We had to content ourselves with several minor targets.

The next day I was sent to the little town of Richemont situated on the Moselle River. It had been heavily shelled, but we found a nice house at the edge of town that had belonged to a schoolteacher who had strong Nazi sympathies. He had wisely fled, but we found wine, chicken, and some second-rate fruit in his yard to supplement our diet. I also uncovered a large Nazi banner that became the only thing I liberated during the war.

We spent the better part of a week at Richemont. Happily, we slept in beds for the first time since leaving England. The Germans did suspect our presence and occasionally fired a few rounds in our direction, but none of them hit the house. We, in turn, sought diligently for their battery. As our jeep was with us, we had a small 20-power telescope available. Once when the German battery was firing, I used it to detect wisps of smoke from a ravine on the far side of the river. I called for fire. One round must have hit an ammunition dump, because there was a tremendous explosion that was also viewed by our air observer. Thereafter, there was no further fire from the German battery.

We were sorry when Lieutenant Yokum, the forward observer of C Battery, and his crew came to relieve us after dark. My men did not want to leave, because it was dangerous riding around the front lines at night. There were many trigger-happy soldiers, and some of the roads had suffered heavily from the war. Besides, our quarters were far more comfortable than the mud hole the battery had been stuck in. I let them persuade me to stay until morning, somewhat to Yokum's and his crew's discomfiture. They had dreamed of having the small house to themselves. The beds had to be shared, and Yokum and I were assigned one by my men who made the necessary dispositions to demonstrate that there was room for us all.

As September of 1944 drew to a close, our battalion moved farther to the south near Doncourt to support the attack on the German forts just to the west of Metz. I established an OP at Villers-aux-Bois, a large farm complex overlooking Gravelotte, where one of the big battles of the Franco-Prussian War had been fought in 1870. The stone building was rectangular in shape, with the living quarters on the west side and the barn on the east. We occupied the hayloft in the latter for a total of two or three weeks. It was our longest stay in any one place and one of our favorites. Hay makes a warm and comfortable bed, the stone walls were two-feet thick, and the observation was quite good. Most important, we were our own bosses. There was no one to tell us what to do.

Isenhour, Speaker, and I were more companions than officer and men, and we were very happy to escape the military rigor of the battery and battalion. By this time, paperback books had been issued to us, and I spent much of my time reading novels. Both of my men smoked, and they left the butts on the window sill. Every day a farm laborer came by to caution us not to burn down the barn and to collect the butts, which he made into cigarettes.

There was a scarcity of ammunition at first, and targets were rare. Driant and the other forts were visible, but the Germans were so well protected in the secure walls that our artillery could do no more than keep them awake. We did watch the Air Force do their bit, but to no avail.

My job was to register the sound and flash unit for the corps. In an ideal situation the guns, the observer, and the target are in a more or less straight line. In such circumstances the observer can easily adjust fire, but in situations in which the angle formed by the guns, target, and observer is over 500 mills, what appears to be a short shot is also far off for deflection. Then it is necessary to employ the Large-T procedure to adjust fire. This was very much a Large-T situation. I had never fired such a mission and am not sure that I had ever seen one fired, but at Fort Sill we had been taught on paper how it was done. Fortunately Captain Kilbourn, who had given me the assignment, had warned me in time. I hastily studied my gunnery book and was ready to go when the time came. I quickly got on the target, the sound and flash unit reported that they had a good adjustment, and Kilbourn passed the word on to me. There must have been observers who were much closer to the line between the guns and the target, and I was flattered to have been chosen.

When I was assigned to the gunnery faculty at Fort Sill after the war in Europe ended, I found that they had ceased to teach Large-T. I was not surprised. I have never heard of another case in which it was employed during the war.

My crew and I were carefully concealed in the hayloft, but there was an infantry company stationed in the farm complex. They were too numerous and too active to remain unnoticed. Not surprisingly, the Germans decided to give us a little trouble. One shell flew over the barn and landed in the courtyard. A second hit just in front of our observation window. It didn't take much of an artilleryman to figure where the next round would go. I pulled my men back from the window just as a shell struck. Our bc scope, through which we had been observing, was knocked down and covered with stone rubble. When I returned during the summer of 1953, the repairs on the barn were still plainly visible.

I began to worry about Christmas. In one letter I suggested that mother buy presents from me to all the family, that Becky get something for mother, and that Becky and mother buy something really nice for Blair. There was much talk about a pearl necklace, but I suggested that they hold back for several months.

Blair's mother had convinced herself that the war would end shortly. She planned to use her husband's influence to bring Blair to Paris so we could be married there. Her proposal was not without its appeal but I suspected that my colleagues in the battalion would take a dim view of my showing up with a wife, thanks to pull, when they had been separated from their families for months. Nevertheless, I was not too worried. In spite of newspaper predictions, I could see no end of the war in sight. Logically, with the great Russian Army advances and the liberation of France, the Germans had lost the war. However, our unconditional surrender policy, coupled with the ridiculous Morgenthau plan, which would have divided Germany into a number of agricultural states, removed any incentive the

Germans might have had to make peace. They bravely fought to the end hoping for a miracle.

On September 24, I reported that the week before I had found a public bathhouse with hot water in a mining town. For 10 francs I had enjoyed the luxury of lounging in a tub. It was the first bath I had had since leaving England a full seven weeks before. The experience was especially delightful because we had been wallowing in mud since the beginning of the month. Once my jeep got stuck in spite of its four-wheel drive. It simply sank into mud up to its running board, and we had had to dismount and push. The battalion was then encamped near Doncourt. I always regretted when I was recalled from my barn and had to cope with this liquid dirt.

On October 8, when I was with the battery, I received a summons to come immediately to battalion headquarters. General Walton H. Walker, the corps commander, was about to arrive to give me the Silver Star for the fight at Mairy. I was muddy all over. The pockets of my field jacket were stuffed, and one bar was missing. I solved that part of my problem by discarding the field jacket. There was still a big tear in one trouser leg, but there was no time to remedy that. I could only hope that under the circumstances no comments would be made.

General Walker was called elsewhere at the last moment, and Brigadier General Julius E. Slack, the corps artillery commander, appeared in his place. Lieutenant Wagner and I were lined up. He was the pilot of one of our liaison planes and received the air medal for flying a certain number of missions. The General's aide read my citation. When he finished, Slack shook my hand and said, "Congratulations for doing your duty." At the time I thought he could have been more loquacious, but on reflection I realize that he had said all that needed to be said. Words like "duty" and "honor" were rarely spoken in those days, but they were understood to be the guiding principles. My actions were based on my fear of not doing my duty, which usually outweighed my fear of the Germans. Today, duty is largely a forgotten word and "rights" has become the key noun in our vocabulary, much to the profit of the lawyers and to the detriment of society.

The one sad aspect of the ceremony was that air observers Lieutenant

Winterer and Sergeant Olliver were not present to receive their medals. They had been shot down by our own artillery five days before. Flying back and forth parallel to our lines, the observers called for fire whenever they found a target. It is easy to see how they might have been in our line of fire.

After the ceremony, I returned to my pup tent and wrote Blair that we had gotten medals. Later, I sent a copy of the citation to my parents. To my horror, I learned after the war that my father had published it and several of my letters in the local weekly newspaper. For some reason he had come to take an interest in his youngest son and one-time problem child. He wrote me two or three times a month and sent letters to several Army headquarters asking for official copies of my citations. General Patton had been his classmate at V.M.I. I don't remember that he ever mentioned him before the war, but he wrote reminding him of their V.M.I. connection and very likely telling him that he had a son in his Army. Busy as he was, Patton replied, on November 28, saying that it

> is always a pleasure to hear from former friends and classmates. Ole V.M.I. has done pretty well in this war, especially when you consider that General [*George C.*] Marshall is its leading alumnus.

My mother and siblings kept all this from me, rightly suspecting that I would be upset and that my weekly letters would degenerate into "I am well. I hope you are well too."

I later learned that I had been recommended for the Silver Star by the infantry officer who had pointed out the German tanks to me. The citation itself was prepared at our battalion headquarters, and no one there had been at the scene of action. In some respects it was not too inaccurate, but if one wrote a history of the battle based on the citation, he would report the story backwards. It asserted that I "corrected the artillery fire until the enemy column was halted, thus enabling infantrymen to close and destroy the enemy armored vehicles." Actually, the infantry company commander halted the column by knocking out the lead tank with a bazooka, and this enabled the artillery to destroy the remaining tanks and armored vehicles. I later learned that another forward observer received the Distinguished Service Cross posthumously for treating the Germans in much the same fashion as I had done. I was more than happy to have received the lesser medal in person.

About this time Ed Seddon, our battery commander, and Gene White, our liaison officer, swapped positions. I thought that both were doing fine jobs where they were, but I suspect that the colonel believed that Gene, a tall Texan who had graduated from Texas A&M, had more drive and determination. Gene was better able to cope with the rough-and-tumble aspects of a battery, while the quieter, cultured Ed could hold down the post of liaison officer as well as he. At the same time, Lee Cass replaced Herbert Strecker as battery executive, again two good men who did fine jobs in those posts. Under Strecker, the battery had fired hundreds of rounds flawlessly on the armored column at Mairy, when the slightest mistake by a gunner could have put a shell on the infantry in the village, or for that matter, on me. Cass was to prove his skill when he went into position on the spur of the moment and broke up a tank attack on a nearby town, and again after the war when Patton gave the highest praise to the battery for its performance in a fire mission.

The newcomers were avid poker players. I had almost never played, and when I had, it was not for money. Nevertheless, to have a decent game, my fellow officers thought it necessary that I take a hand. I agreed to be a good sport, but quit when I had lost my monthly allowance, in spite of offers to lend me any amount. The stakes were high, but the others let me win occasionally to prolong the game. Once I was dealt two pair. I discarded a card, and the one I drew gave me a full house. My face clearly revealed what had happened, but the others matched my raises. I pocketed $63, which had a buying power of about ten times that amount today. This assured a longer game, but soon the pot and my allowance was back in their hands.

I have called this phase of my military life the "phantom" war. Neither bombs nor rockets had threatened us during our stay in western England, and the dash across France had been a lark. My job to register the sound and flash unit and the victory at Mairy, the chance shell that had hit an ammunition dump and knocked out an enemy battery at Richemont, and my receiving the Silver Star had marked my only triumphs in the war thus far. Neither I nor any of my men had received a scratch. Sure, we had been hot and dirty during the early fair weather and cold, dirty, and wet when the rains came. Throughout we had suffered from acute boredom. Yet, our minor miseries would have soon been forgotten if the war had come to an end then. It would have been remembered only as a happy, exciting experience that every man should enjoy once in his lifetime. But a change was about to take place. The real war was about to begin.

This page and next: Battery B, 949 Field Artillery Battalion, Fort Bragg, North Carolina, *ca.* December 1943. L to r, front row: Sergeants Golos, Knitter, Lieutenants Heilman, Major, Seddon, Strecker, Hawks, Sergeants Roman, Parada; second row: no. 12, Sergeant Speaker; no. 21, Corporal Isenhour; third row: no. 13, Corporal Bradshaw, no. 17, Sergeant Currie.

Eugene M. White, Jr.

Ed Seddon (l) and William J. Hawks.

Captain Don Kilbourn at Adolph Hitler's mountain retreat, Eagle's Nest, near Berchtesgaden, in the summer of 1945.

Luxembourg during the Battle of the Bulge. The tents are covering the ammunition.

At the Battle of the Bulge. The tent at the gun squad had just been collapsed. The pipe carried the smoke of the stove up and out of the tent.

Lieutenant J. Russell Major on the road to Wintersport, Germany, February 5, 1945.

Schimpach Station, taken in the summer 1953. On January 15, 1945, Major came down the wooded, snow-covered hill on the right and was shot in the wrist while standing on the tracks in the foreground. The Germans were in the woods at the far end of the tracks.

Left: Lee Cass (l) and Gene White.

Below: Lieutenant Colonel Russell M. Frink in a most uncharacteristic pose, May 12, 1945.

Chapter 5

The Real War:
The Moselle and the Saar

B Y THE SECOND WEEK OF NOVEMBER 1944, the
Third Army was ready to strike again. Sufficient supplies
had been collected to take Metz and to rush on to the Saar
River. The previous assaults on the Metz forts had been
costly failures. General Walker wisely decided on new tactics. The 90th Infantry Division was directed to establish a bridgehead over the Moselle River to the north of Thionville and then to
drive to the southeast. The 5th Infantry Division already had a small
bridgehead over the Moselle to the south of Metz, and it was to drive
to the northeast and link up with the 90th. When they did so, the
Metz garrison would be surrounded unless they abandoned the forts
before the vise was closed.

We greatly outnumbered the Germans, and many of their troops
were inexperienced or older men. They did have a most potent ally,
the weather. It had rained almost daily for over a month, and the
ground was thoroughly soaked. Instead of clearing for our assault,
the clouds opened up more than ever. The Moselle was transformed
into a torrent, and it spread over the surrounding plains, a mile or

more wide in places. Snow flurries reminded us that the water was cold and winter was coming. The elements would prove to be as difficult to overcome as the Germans.

By this time, I had adopted the costume that I was to wear until warm weather returned. An officer's overcoat and raincoat did not reach the knees. Water ran off them to the trouser legs and down into the boots. Somewhere I found a raincoat to which about 18 inches had been added so that it reached the tops of my boots. It served to ward off the rain and as an ideal windbreaker. Beneath it I wore every article of clothing that I could find, starting with a field jacket and including the inevitable necktie. It did not solve all my problems, but it was the best solution I could manage during the war.

The adverse weather caused another change. In the charge across France, I had slept in the open or in a pup tent. I now abandoned the latter and joined White and the headquarters personnel in a wall tent when I was with the battery. Similar tents were provided the crew of each gun and the other sections of the battery. Somewhere the men in each tent had found stoves. It is amazing how a stove with only a piece of canvas between it and the elements can keep a large area warm. As long as one could enjoy its shelter, one could cope with the bitter cold of a European winter. The trouble was that my men and I were not able to spend much time with the battery.

The 949th Field Artillery was among a number of battalions assigned to support the 90th Division. We moved to a secret assembly area just after dark on November 2. On the 8th, White was sent to man an OP leaving me in command of the battery. We moved the batteries forward after darkness that same day to support the infantry when they jumped off at 3:30 the next morning.

Our battery had been assigned a pretty green field, but when we moved into position that unusually dark and rainy night, we discovered that beneath the green sward lay several feet of mud. Some of our vehicles got stuck and had to be winched into position. One of our ammunition trucks broke through the little bridge leading onto the field and turned over. Every time a track (tractor) moved to correct the situation, it cut the telephone lines. The one line that escaped was to the battalion. Soon the colonel was on the line asking when we would be ready to fire. By the time the infantry jumped off, we were all set. Cass was unimpressed by my performance and said he would rather handle the battery alone when

From United States Army in World War II: The European Theater of Operations — The Lorraine Campaign, by Hugh M. Cole (Washington, D.C.: Historical Division, Dept. of the Army, 1950), Map XXX.

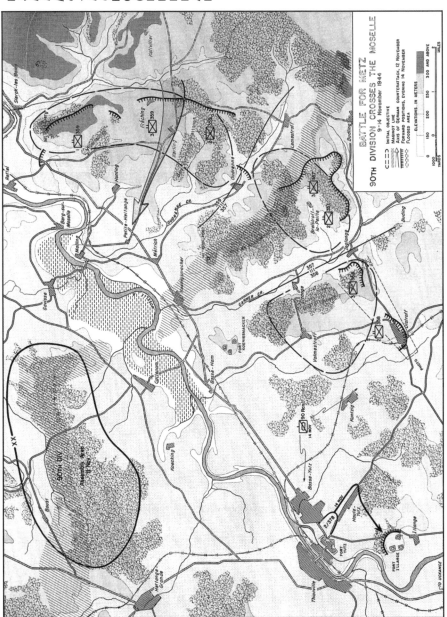

White was away. Perhaps I could have done better, but to occupy a mud hole on a dark rainy night in a total blackout after a bridge collapsed was not an easy thing to do.

The whole episode was ironic. I had been assigned to teach tactics at Fort Sill because of the skill I had exhibited as the executive when we moved into position and had critiqued students on their actions as battery commanders at least a hundred times. Nothing is easier than putting a battery in position under ordinary conditions, but thereafter I went with White or acted on my own when the battery was on the move.

The 90th achieved tactical surprise. The Germans did not believe that we would be so bold as to attack when the river was so high. Our infantry enjoyed initial success, but it was very difficult to get reinforcements and supplies to them. On November 11, the Germans launched several counterattacks and recaptured the village of Kerling about three miles from the river. At this point, I was given the mission of establishing an Observation Post on the high ground near Kerling that was visible from one occupied by Lieutenant MacClintock, who had joined the infantry the day before. We were to survey in targets, an exercise that had worked beautifully at Fort Sill but never for me in combat. The Germans always seemed to occupy some of the necessary high ground. Then, too, both OP's had to have good observation of the same target area and their exact location had to be known.

I moved on to the village of Gavisse on the temporary banks of the flooded river. As the bridge was not yet in, I left Isenhour with instructions to follow with the jeep as soon as possible. Speaker and I then waded waist deep in the flooded river to a point where the engineers had boats to ferry us to the other side. German artillery shelled our boats, but I never saw them score a hit.

When we reached Malling on the east side, freezing and soaking wet, we set out on foot for Petite-Hettange about a mile and a half away. Here I found MacClintock still a little shaken from his narrow escape during the counterattacks. Darkness was coming, and we found space in a house with a warm stove. I placed my boots close to it to be sure that they would be dry by morning, and we moved to the basement where we would be safer from enemy artillery. Around 4 a.m., we were awakened by artillery and small-arms fire. We went upstairs, and I found that my boots had curled up and cracked because they had been too close to the stove. I could barely get them on. Mac and I ran across the street to the 2nd Battalion headquarters to see if we could help. By that time bullets were whizzing down the street, and the counterattack had reached the crossroads several hundred yards to the east.

All was confusion. The infantry had no defense against tanks except bazookas and what support they could get from the artillery on the other side of the river. At the critical moment, two of our tank destroyers came charging up the road from Malling. We gave a mighty cheer. They were the deciding factor in halting the counterattack. The engineers had completed the bridge just in time in spite of unbelievable difficulties. Unhappily, the German artillery knocked it out before further help could come.

After the counterattack had been repulsed, Speaker and I set out on foot to find the 3rd Battalion of the 359th Infantry Regiment. We finally located it in the early afternoon in a woods northwest of Kerling. It was in sad shape; one company did not have a single officer left. Indeed, six of the nine infantry battalions in the 90th Division had lost half their fighting strength. The enemy frequently shelled the woods. We dug in and spent a freezing night. We had no blankets, my clothes had not yet dried from our river crossing, and my warped boots had worn blisters on my feet.

Around noon the next day, November 13, we retook Kerling without firing a shot. The Germans had abandoned the village. Our men must have been caught by surprise when the Germans had counterattacked several days before. Two or three of them were killed putting their boots on. In death, they still sat in an upright position.

By this time the bridge had been repaired, and I had Speaker radio "Ike" Isenhour to join us at Kerling. Several infantrymen overheard us and wondered if we were not contacting the other soldier, General Eisenhower, of that name. When Ike arrived, we pulled blankets, dry clothes, and food from the jeep. I spent the afternoon looking for a suitable OP without success. That evening I was ordered to return to the battalion that had just crossed the river. I had accomplished nothing.

On November 19, the forces of the 5th and 90th Divisions joined. The Germans who had not already escaped were cut off, and soon the garrisons in Metz and the forts were forced to surrender. The 90th Division, with the 949th Field Artillery Battalion in support, dashed on toward the Saar River.

Next, I was assigned to the 3rd Battalion of the 357th Regiment as an observer. On November 26, we crossed a small stream and took a village just over the French-German border. The battalion operational narrative recorded that Lieutenant Major and party "were the first members of the battalion to put foot on German soil, doing so late this afternoon." The Germans took a dim view of our presence, and we were confronted with a considerable amount of artillery fire.

I believe it was at this time that I was attached to an infantry company dug in on an exposed, barren hillside. I told Isenhour to remain in a village with the jeep and to come get us after dark. Speaker, his radio, and I found a good foxhole someone else had dug and crawled in to spend a very long day. Every few minutes the Germans dropped a shell on the company. As long as one stayed in his foxhole, he was in no danger unless they got a direct hit. Only once did this happen, and we heard a loud cry for aid men. Shell fragments made life outside one's foxhole dangerous. To avoid unnecessary exposure, we urinated in our empty waterproof K ration boxes and threw the contents out on the ground. There we remained in the rain, fog, and cold. Visibility was poor, and we never saw a target. It was then that I decided to study contemporary history to find out how and why we had gotten into this mess. Finally, darkness came and Isenhour picked us up as directed.

On November 29, we entered a small town that was being heavily shelled. I left our jeep on a street where it was protected from artillery fire by buildings and established an OP in a house on the high ground at the edge of the town. The weather was very cold and wet. I let my men make a fire out of the furniture in the house rather than insist that they forage for wood amid the shrapnel flying through the streets. We found no targets, and our OP in the frame building was far from safe. We had to occupy the upstairs to get better observation, while the infantry huddled in the basement, only a foot or so of which was above the ground. Two shells hit the downstairs, and then one struck the narrow opening in the basement, killing one man. Although in the most exposed position, we got off scot-free. However, our jeep was less fortunate. A tank had backed over some mines beside it. The tankers had been blown to the top of a barn, and my jeep had been destroyed. Happily, it was immediately replaced.

The next day we moved to another village, and I found an Observation Post in a house on a hillside. The Germans began to shell us with a huge gun mounted on a railroad car. Hidden in a railway tunnel when not firing, it could not be hit by our Air Force or artillery. When Speaker went to get some water from a nearby well, one of the shells landed at the far end of the village. He came back panting, "Did you see that 88mm shell that hit right beside me?" We had a hard time convincing him that it had been a far larger shell that had landed a half-mile away. The concussion of this mammoth gun was many times larger than anything in our arsenal.

At dawn the next day, I set up an OP in a woods overlooking the Saar River. The pillboxes of the Siegfried Line were plainly in view across the swollen stream. I fired a number of missions, but our howitzers did little damage. Several 155mm self-propelled guns that fired point-blank at a distance of about 2,000 yards had given a better account of themselves. The Air Force also got in the game. Their bombs landed on both sides of the river. No one on our side was hurt, and as far as we could see the Germans also got away with no casualties.

On December 3, I was recalled and rejoined our battery in a wooded area. Enemy artillery fired a few rounds at us, but what made us maddest was that one of our own planes strafed our position. That evening the pilot had the gall to telephone to learn whether he had hit anyone. He was clearing his guns and had not noticed that we were in the woods until too late. Imagine clearing your guns in friendly territory! Fortunately no one was hit, but one bullet went through a tent.

At 4 a.m., on December 6, the 90th Division launched an assault across the Saar and into the Siegfried Line. The German defenses here were stronger than anywhere else on the western front. I was assigned to Company F, 2nd Battalion of the 357th Infantry Regiment. Since it would be a difficult mission, I decided to take three men with me instead of the usual two. Isenhour and Speaker were weighed down with the radio, and I carried maps, field glasses, and other equipment and had to be free to move quickly. Hence, I added Private L. to our party to carry some K rations and blankets. Colen M. Hoyle, a 21-year-old North Carolinian, drove us to the 2nd Battalion headquarters after dark on the 5th and was to return to the battery the next morning. I got up about 3 a.m. to prepare for the crossing and found L. doubled up with pain. I thought that the odds were two-to-one that he was faking, but I could not risk taking a man who might be sick on such a difficult mission. Hoyle went in his place.

The liaison officer who was to guide us to our company got lost in the total blackout. The first light of dawn was just breaking when we found the place of embarkation. The infantry had long since departed, as had the engineers who had ferried them across the Saar. However, they had left their boats. I met another forward observer and his crew who had not found his infantry company either. We decided to join forces, borrow one of the engineer assault boats, and cross the flooded river on our own.

With the advantage of hindsight, it was a crazy thing to have done. We did not know exactly where the infantry had gone or what was on the other side of the Saar. My only thought was that we were supposed to be with the infantry, and they were certain to need us sooner or later. We eight, armed only with six carbines and two pistols, therefore set out to assault the mighty Siegfried Line. The flooded river was our first problem, but I exuded confidence, as I had paddled many a mile in a canoe on the Shenandoah River back home. I quickly found that a canoe and an assault boat are not propelled forward and guided the same way. When we reached the main channel of the rapidly flowing, flooded river, our boat spun around several times. We finally straightened it out and reached land near a blown-out railroad bridge.

While our men unloaded our gear, the other lieutenant and I went forward a few yards to reconnoiter. There was no sign of our infantry, but the Germans quickly made their presence known. A blast of machine-gun fire came from a pillbox beside the railroad causeway about 25 yards away. The other officer jumped beneath the concrete arch of the bridge. Unhappily the blown-out railroad track lay turned on its side between me and safety. I tried to squeeze between its ties. I could feel the heat of the bullets as they whizzed by my neck. Apparently the pillbox prevented the German from depressing his weapon enough to hit me. At length, I wiggled between the ties — it paid to be thin — and found safety under the arch. We called back to our men who had taken cover behind the river bank and another railroad arch. They were all accounted for except Hoyle. I suspect that he had been hit just as he lifted the rations and blankets from the boat and sank with his burden without making a sound. We liked to believe that when the fire started, he had dropped his load in the river and had swum back to the other shore. He was a strong swimmer, but the water was very cold, and it would have been a miracle if he reached safety. Hoyle was very popular, and his wife was about to have a baby. It encouraged us to hope that he might be alive.

We were trapped. The Germans tried to throw hand grenades under the arch, but they could not reach us. We could only wait until help came. About an hour later, an infantry company appeared and was ferried across to our blown-out bridge. The Germans in the pillbox must have fled, for we heard no more of them.

After making a thorough search for Hoyle, we moved on with the infantrymen. We had not far to go. Instead of walking down the railroad tracks to Dillingen about a mile away, the company sought the protection of the causeway to shield them from occasional sniper fire. Soon, they stopped altogether in the mud. I suppose they planned to wait until nightfall when the snipers would be less dangerous. In the meantime, they were subject to mortar fire and trench foot, due to the inclement weather, which cost us far more men than enemy action. I shivered, cursed, and lingered with them for hours.

At length, I learned that the assault companies had captured the northern suburbs of the town. Then a lone infantry lieutenant appeared, walking down the track ignoring the occasional sniper. His bold action taught me a lesson. It was less costly to push forward than to lie and wait. We were more likely to survive and accomplish our mission by following his example than by remaining where we were. I mounted the track and walked to Dillingen, followed by my men.

Around 4 p.m., we reached F Company lodged in a house at the edge of town. The house was so crowded that it was difficult to find a place to stretch out. The infantrymen built fires in the room. The smoke was so bad that our eyes hurt and we could barely breathe. Nevertheless, the room was dry, and my men and I found a quilt that we shared. Our own blankets and food had been lost, but the men gave each of us one K ration box. It was the only food we had that day. After getting the plan of attack from the company commander, I joined my men, cold, wet, and shivering on the floor. We were too miserable to get much sleep.

We were scheduled to jump off at 4 a.m. the next morning, but as usual the darkness and confusion led to delays. We entered a woods and advanced up a draw. Around daybreak we came upon a pillbox that opened fire on us. The infantry wanted me to knock it out. I was loathe to try. It is difficult to pinpoint an enemy target in a woods, especially when you do not know your exact location. More important, one rarely gets a direct hit with a howitzer, and even if one does, it won't destroy a pillbox. All I could hope to do was to neutralize the garrison while the company closed in. My men set up the radio while I tried to figure our location and where the target was. Just as we were ready to adjust fire, another burst came from the pillbox. The infantrymen scampered through the woods. As we had no intention of facing the Germans alone, we dismantled the radio and joined our fleeing comrades as fast as we could.

Our companions solved the pillbox problem by bypassing it. The next company that came along was left with the chore of taking it out. Finally, we reached high ground and settled down for the night. In the river crossing and the fight that followed, F Company had abandoned its bazookas and all but one of its machine guns. Half the company had been lost, more to exposure in the cold weather than to enemy action. Only one officer remained. With little besides their rifles, they were in no condition to defend themselves against the counterattack that was almost sure to come. Therefore, I asked our battalion to fire one round every minute during the night on a series of points from which a German attack might come. I chose spots about 100 yards from our position to prevent them from slipping under our covering fire. The enemy did counterattack in some areas, but either through luck or their discouragement by our artillery fire, they left us alone.

I was cold, wet, and exhausted. Instead of digging my foxhole in firm ground, I bored into the side of an embankment made for a dirt road used for logging. The work went fast in the soft soil. Soon it was finished, and I crawled in, placed my map case over my face to prevent grains of dirt and drops of water from falling on me, and went to sleep listening to shells whining overhead and crashing into the trees. Sometime during the night I was awakened when my foxhole collapsed on me. My map case provided a little pocket of air so that I did not breathe in dirt, but about two feet of dirt was on me. I could not move, and it was only with great effort that I could breathe. I called for Speaker and Isenhour and I yelled for help, but no one came. I could hear our shells exploding and could not see why no one could hear me. Finally I gave up. I dared not go to sleep for fear that without special effort, the weight of the dirt would stop me from breathing. I determined to keep my mind so occupied that I would stay awake until dawn came and I was found.

It is said that there are no atheists in foxholes. This is not true, at least in my case. My brother and three sisters were staunch Episcopalians, but in spite of my mother's efforts, I had always been indifferent to religion. If there was a good and all-powerful God, I asked myself, why this war?

Why had a fine young man like Hoyle been almost certainly killed? Why was I buried alive in this remote part of Europe? The answer seemed clear. There was no such God. I have since learned that my theology was un-original and simplistic, but it was the best I could do under the circumstances.

Most of my thoughts were on Blair. What would it be like to be married to her? What delights were in store for me? These were dreams that I could imagine over and over again while I struggled to stay awake. Then I realized once more that if I could hear our shells, somebody must be able to hear my calls for help. I began shouting again. This time Speaker recognized his name, and he and Isenhour dug me out. They literally had to lift me from my grave. I could not stand. I imagine that I had been buried for five or six hours, as dawn was just breaking on one of the shortest days of the year. A number of soldiers said they had heard me, but the dirt had muffled my voice and they could not understand. They had assumed that my calls for help were the cries of Germans wounded by our artillery fire.

I ate my one box of K ration for the day and staggered along with the infantry as they advanced about a thousand yards to the end of the woods. An open, treeless field lay beyond. Throughout the day one target appeared after another. German companies of infantry were retreating from the front. As they went single file about five or six yards apart, they were not especially lucrative targets, but we had plenty of ammunition and I fired away. Once a horse-drawn artillery battery appeared. I sent a few innocent animals to their graves and perhaps some cannoneers to accompany them. Battalion headquarters asked where I had found so many targets, and the After Action Report noted that "Lt. Major our observer across the Saar River had a field day when he caught a large number of enemy infantry as well as a horse drawn column in the open."

I was after bigger game. We could hear an enemy artillery battery firing from the woods between us and our battalion. In another part of the woods, German mortars were very active. I determined to climb a tree at the edge of the woods, pinpoint the location of these two targets, and knock them out. A handful of Germans were in a trench 120 yards from my position. I thought it wise to cow them before making my ascent. I should have adjusted with one gun; however, I was so accustomed to using the whole battery that I did so again. On the third volley, one round fired short and landed about 25 yards behind me in the midst of the infantry. It was a miracle that no one was hurt. I suppose the guilty gunner had decreased instead of increased the range or had failed to level the bubble, and the battery executive had not caught his error. Artillery observers who fired short were not popular with the infantry, and I expect that I lost some of the good will I had earned by saving their necks the night before.

Everything seemed ready. It was my one chance during the war to be a hero and to make a real difference. The German artillery and mortars were wreaking havoc among our troops. I remembered that General Kilbourne, the superintendent of V.M.I., had won the Medal of Honor for climbing a telegraph pole to restore communications in full view of the enemy. It was then I discovered that I was so exhausted that I could not climb the tree. I still do not see how I could have been so tired that I was unable to muster the strength for this one last effort, but I could not. Dejected, I reached for my canteen. It was empty. A shell fragment had pierced it, and all the water had escaped. The fragment must have come from the short round, but I do not remember whether I was wearing the canteen at the time, or whether it had been hit when I laid it on the ground preparatory to climbing the tree. I saved my punctured canteen as a keepsake and borrowed a full one from a dead G.I.

As darkness approached, we withdrew to where we had spent the preceding night. This time Isenhour and Speaker set about preparing a real foxhole for the three of us. They cut branches to make a roof and to secure the sides, all to no avail. When it was ready, we received orders to pull back. Our lines were overextended, and we needed to consolidate to meet a possible counterattack.

F Company was assigned a pillbox. It was so crowded that we had to sit up, and as usual the infantry began to build fires to heat coffee or to warm their hands. How they could stand the smoke, I do not know. It was another cold, miserable, and hungry night.

My concerned men had asked me to request to be relieved. I hated the thought, but I gradually came to realize that I was no longer capable of doing the job. In fairness to the infantry, I ought to be replaced. Furthermore, our radio batteries were almost dead after a day of constant missions. I humbled my pride and asked to be replaced.

The next morning we set out for Dillingen and quickly ran into trouble. The Germans were counterattacking in a few areas, and there were snipers

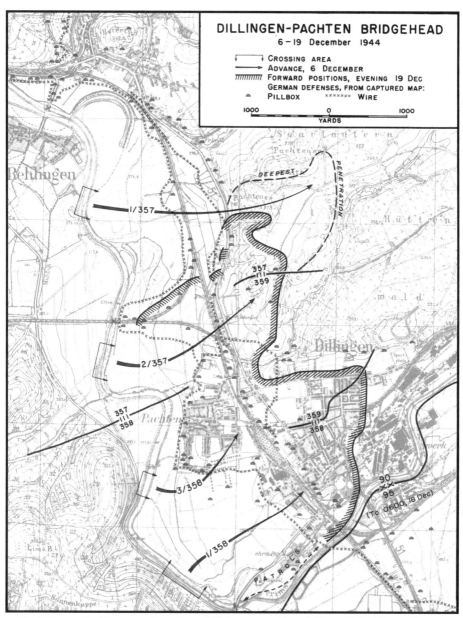

The Dillingen-Pachten area where Russell Major was positioned. (From *United States Army in World War II: The European Theater of Operations — The Lorraine Campaign*, by Hugh M. Cole (Washington, D.C.: Historical Division, Dept. of the Army, 1950), Map XLI.

everywhere. We had to cross an open field under fire. Speaker and Isen-hour suggested that we abandon the radio and make a run for it. They each carried a section that weighed about 46 pounds. My first reaction was to say, "No! No!" Then reason came to the fore. I was too weak to offer to carry even one section. The batteries were dead, so we had no way to call for fire to help the infantry, and the lives of my men were certainly more valuable than a $1,000 radio. Even without this weight, we walked rather than ran over the 220-yard open stretch.

A little later we met the division reserve that was then being committed. During an artillery barrage, I found myself in a crater with a sergeant of the advancing reserve regiment. I must have looked pretty awful, because he offered me a D ration, which consisted of a hard chunk of unsweetened chocolate designed to provide energy in extreme cases. He insisted that he didn't like it. I was so hungry that I accepted, never thinking to ask why he was carrying the chocolate if he had no intention of eating it. This has always troubled me, because within 12 hours I was safe and he was still in danger.

When we reached Dillingen on December 9, we found part of it in flames. A serious counterattack was expected. I located my replacement and discovered that he had not brought his radio because he planned to use mine. I was amazed. He and his crew had been ferried across the river by the engineers, and there had been no difficulties in walking up the railroad tracks to the town. I suppose he anticipated more problems than he encountered. In any case, it was the only time during the war I know of when the relief team expected to use the equipment of its predecessor.

I was interviewed by a full colonel about conditions at the front. He soon realized that I was not coherent enough to give accurate information.

We waited until after dark when the engineers carried the wounded to the opposite shore and caught a ride. A jeep was waiting for us, and we reached battalion headquarters around 10:30 p.m. to make a report. I wor-ried about the reception I would get. I had substituted Hoyle for Private L. at the cost of the former's life. I had asked to be relieved, the only time to my knowledge that one of our observers did so during the war. I had dis-carded my radio. There was not much in this to be proud of.

My reception could not have been warmer. The horrors at the front had filtered back to the battalion. I was told that I had been the only functional forward observer in the area of the 357th Infantry Regiment. The others had been knocked out or had abandoned their radios. One battalion had lost five forward observer teams. My superiors may have magnified the actual losses, but they believed them to be true. By comparison we looked pretty good. We had lost only one man and had knocked out several hundred enemy infantry and a few guns. By our prearranged fires we may have prevented a counterattack on the night of December 7.

Someone offered me a big drink of scotch, but Captain Bick, our medic, put a stop to that after one swallow. Another officer, I believe Captain Kilbourn, gave me his bed. This was more to the point. It was agreed that my men and I would rest at headquarters where we would be more comfortable than in tents with the battery. It was only recently when I saw the After Action Report that I discovered that Captain Bick wanted us to stay at headquarters where he could keep an eye on us. I suppose he thought we might have psychological problems.

I slept for 36 of the next 48 hours. In my waking moments, I spent most of my time eating. For four days I had had only one K ration box a day. After our recovery, we returned to the battery. I told Captain White of our adventures. He grabbed pencil and paper and recommended each of us for a medal. When we were transferred from the 20th Corps to the 8th Corps at the beginning of the Battle of the Bulge, in December 1944, the recommendations were moved as well.

On March 1, Colonel John B. Horton, the assistant corps artillery commander, approved a recommendation that I be given an oak leaf cluster to the Silver Star and forwarded it to 8th Corps Headquarters. At this point the recommendation was lost, as were those of my men. The 90th Infantry Division was ordered to abandon its bridgehead soon after the Battle of the Bulge began. There was nothing to show for our efforts or to justify the deaths of those who had fought so hard.

However, one act of justice did take place. Private L. had a miraculous recovery after we had crossed the Saar. He drove the jeep back to the battery and there learned that Hoyle, who had replaced him, was missing in action. L. had always been a loner with few if any friends, while Hoyle was universally popular. He was more or less put in Coventry. Perhaps for this reason he did not object when an order came to transfer some hardened veterans to the infantry and he was volunteered. We never heard from him again.

Chapter 6

The Real War: The Bulge

I WAS ACTING AS LIAISON OFFICER at the 241st Field Artillery Battalion headquarters on December 17, 1944, when news began to pour in about the German counteroffensive. Their advance into Belgium and Luxembourg had forced a "bulge" in Allied lines, hence the action, starting in December 1944 and ending in January 1945, has been named the "Battle of the Bulge."

Some officers in the battalion had at least indirect contact with Third Army headquarters and reported that the enemy initiative was seen as an opportunity. The German army had denuded their strength along the Siegfried Line to launch the drive. It was only necessary to surround them by cutting them off at the base, destroy them in the open, and then break through the undermanned West Wall as the line was called. Unhappily, General Eisenhower insisted on his usual policy of pushing the Germans back on all fronts, and no serious effort was made to cut them off at the base as General Patton urged.

That evening I received orders to relieve our forward observer who was across the Saar River. On the 19th, we made preparations for our march to Luxembourg, and we departed just after midnight.

This was part of General Patton's famous promise to disengage enough forces from the Saar River front to put three divisions in action on the southern flank of the Bulge in three days and to make a coordinated attack with six divisions in six days. It was an unprecedented claim and an unbelievable feat, which the fast-moving Patton accomplished in spite of bad weather that included snow from the 22nd on.

During our long march, I was part of the reconnaissance team. The inadequate road net was packed with vehicles heading north. There were frequent delays and much confusion. Often the battalion moved at night in blackout, and the reconnaissance group spent the days looking for concentration areas for the next move. We were assigned to support the 104th Infantry Regiment of the 26th Infantry Division and received our first fire missions early on the evening of December 22 when the division went into action.

I don't remember what I did the next two days, but on Christmas Day I was sent forward to join the infantry. On the way, I passed a captain directing his battery into position. I gave my usual snappy salute, and the captain yelled, "Hey, Russell." It was Jim Cheatham whom I had not seen since he went through BOC at Fort Sill. We talked of old times for a few minutes. He had recently seen Clyde Hooker who was in a 12th Corps artillery battalion in the Third Army. I started to ask him what time he was serving the turkey dinner we had been promised, but thought better of it. My men were standing around listening. I didn't want to get their hopes up. I could not see how I could tell the infantry we had been invited to dinner and would be back in a couple of hours. "Hope nothing happens while we are gone," I told Cheatham as we departed. The turkey dinners people at home were assured that we were all getting could not be served in the front lines. I might add that during the course of the war, neither I nor any of my men participated in a special feast at Thanksgiving or Christmas, or saw a USO show.

We were lucky to share a room with the infantry that evening in Grosbous, Luxembourg. In addition to Speaker and Isenhour, who nearly always accompanied me, I brought William J. Jedrzjeck, whom we called "Jed," as the driver. He was another fine soldier, completely reliable whether things were hot or calm.

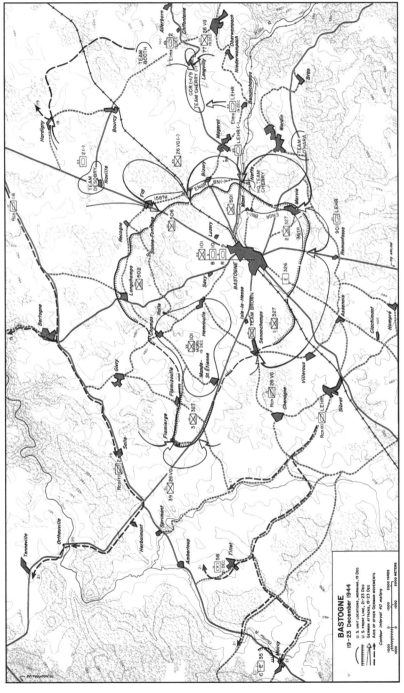

BASTOGNE
19–23 December 1944

From *United States Army in World War II: The European Theater of Operations — The Ardennes: Battle of the Bulge*, by Hugh M. Cole (Washington, D.C.: Historical Division, Dept. of the Army, 1965), Map VI.

Christmas boxes had been flowing to me from family and friends. Most consisted of candy, brownies, cookies, and the like, but I also remember nuts from Blair, and they were usually all devoured upon arrival. For Christmas dinner I could supply the four of us with canned beef, preserves, and crackers, as well as noodle soup from Blair to supplement our K rations. Two things made the evening particularly enjoyable; somewhere we had acquired two bottles of excellent white wine, and our room was equipped with a stove. We "didn't get cold at all during the night," I wrote my mother. "All in all it was a very enjoyable day."

Two gifts that Christmas especially touched me. We Majors had continued to hang up our stockings on Christmas Eve even after the youngest of us had ceased to be a true believer in Santa Claus for a good 15 years. The fruit, nuts, and candy were replaced annually, but after the stockings had been opened before breakfast, my frugal mother gathered up the toys to save for the next Christmas. Most famous of these recycled gifts was a wooden snake. There was always much speculation over who would get it each year. That Christmas of 1944 it was one of my gifts. I regret that I somehow lost it, and the snake passed into family folklore.

The second gift was from Polly Branham, a friend of my parents, who had been my English teacher in the 8th or 9th grade. In addition to some cookies, she sent a paperback book of verses. I have never cared much for poetry. To be poetry, I thought it had to rhyme, and if it did rhyme, it rarely made much sense to me. Still, there were exceptions. Edgar Allen Poe was my favorite. I have always marveled at his ability to create the desired atmosphere by his choice of words. With Poe's exception, my favorites were heroic poems such as Lord Alfred Tennyson's "The Charge of the Light Brigade," and those of defiance such as William Ernest Henley's "Invictus." I could still remember many lines my English teacher Dodo Dillard made me memorize at V.M.I. I kept the book of verses in my knapsack and occasionally read them throughout the remainder of the war. Unlike the snake, the little volume somehow survived, and I still have it in my possession.

On December 26, we moved to Eschdorf, Luxembourg, which had just been taken after much hard fighting. It was a small town whose principal road led a mile or so across a plateau and then plunged down into a deep gorge made by the Sure River. After passing through the picturesque village of Esch-sur-Sure, it climbed sharply to the crest of the plateau on the other side and ran along high ground cut by deep ravines to Wiltz, the division objective. My observer team was to join the infantry, lying in the snow overlooking the gorge, and to assist them in crossing the river. The Sure was never more than 25 yards wide, and it was not flooded — a welcome change. Still, the gorge was the most precipitous I have ever seen, and only the swiftness of the water had prevented it from freezing. The prospects were not inviting, but there was no alternative but to move forward.

Our jeep was parked on the heavily traveled main road leading toward Wiltz. We decided to pull into a side street to unload. Jed and I got in front and Isenhour crawled in the back, but Speaker hopped up on the motor. I ought to have ordered him to get in or walk, but we were going no more than 50 feet, and the infantry had been wandering safely around the village all afternoon. Just after we turned onto the side street, our jeep hit a mine. Jed and Ike were unhurt, and I escaped with a cut on my forehead; but Speaker's leg below the knee was blown off. He lay writhing on the ground where he had been thrown. Ike, ever observant, had noted that there was an aid station at the corner. While Jed and I stood helpless, he rushed back; and in a matter of seconds, two aid men appeared with a stretcher. We accompanied them to the aid station and watched as the medics did all they could. Finally they asked us to leave. I must have contacted the battalion, and a vehicle was sent to take us back to the battery. We arrived after dark — never had we been so full of gloom.

The next morning I received a telephone call saying that Captain Zeller, the motor maintenance officer, was coming with a wrecker, and I was to take him to the jeep. It was a clear, cold day. We stood beside the wreck. Simultaneously, we saw Speaker's leg lying in stark simplicity in the snow. I remembered how he had loved to dance. Once when he had found a top hat and a cane, he had marched back and forth like a vaudeville actor. As these scenes passed through my mind, I heard Zeller say, "Poor fellow, he won't need it anymore." It was then I learned that Speaker had died during the night. He was a brave and conscientious soldier, an excellent radio technician, and, above all, a wonderful friend and companion. He was sorely missed.

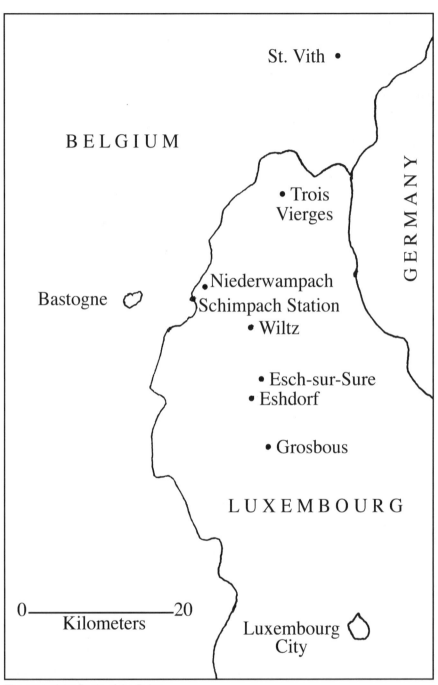

The area of the Battle of the Bulge.

The battalion left us alone in our grief for several days. A chaplain performed an appropriate service, and another chapter in my wartime odyssey came to an end. I had lost two fine men that month. As I took only two or three with me on a mission, the casualty rate had been high indeed.

Our battalion displaced forward to a point not far from Eschdorf overlooking the Sure gorge so as to better support the infantry. On December 26, Bastogne, Belgium, had been relieved by the 4th Armored Division, and the 26th Division had occupied much of the plateau on the other side of the Sure River but still had not taken Wiltz.

On December 30, I was ordered forward as an observer with an infantry company. I took Raymond H. Bradshaw with me as my radio operator. He was a very tall, thin, but unusually strong man who had worked in the oil fields near Tulsa, Oklahoma. He had been called up long before the war and was more than ready to escape the Army by the time I joined the battalion. I suspect he knew his radio as well as Speaker, and he certainly had the necessary courage, but I never felt as much at home with him. On this as on nearly all other occasions, the faithful Isenhour was a member of my team.

I was sent forward and found the infantry dug into the snow. I soon realized that the company commander spent most of his time in his foxhole. He apparently anticipated my concern, for he volunteered that so many company commanders had been killed that they had been ordered not to expose themselves more than absolutely necessary. An officer had never been more obedient. The same rule apparently did not apply to the junior lieutenant in the company, who had been sent with a platoon to clear a nearby woods and to perform other dangerous missions. There was bad feeling between the two. The junior lieutenant obviously thought that the company commander was trying to get him killed, while the latter considered him a no-good coward.

It was not a congenial atmosphere, so I eventually moved to a nearby haystack. Our location put us at the mercy of German patrols and their infantry that we could plainly see a few hundred yards away. On the other hand, we not only escaped an unpleasant situation between the officers of our infantry, but also gained a warm, soft place to sleep. A bed dug deep into a haystack might not be the best protection from a German 88mm gun, but warmth and comfort more than compensated for any danger. As it turned out, the threat came from a mortar.

From my OP we could see the outskirts of Wiltz, our long-elusive objective. The next day I registered the battalion and fired on enemy infantrymen, some in a house and some in vehicles. They were not important targets, but they were enough to make the Germans mad. I had evidently been spotted as the guilty observer. Soon mortar shells began to fall near us. A mortar can shoot almost directly into the air and can come down into any foxhole. I had to press as tightly as I could against the haystack to avoid being hit, but I did not escape a burning sensation on my neck each time a round was fired. Only after the Germans had given up did I discover that the mortar shells had exploded when they hit a tree right behind me and fragments had penetrated my raincoat. Occasionally one of the fragments worked its way out from that time until the end of the war.

That night, New Year's Eve, we were provided spectacular fireworks by our battalion. The newly invented posit fuse caused a shell to explode at a predetermined height above the ground. When coupled with white phosphorus, a colorful explosion appeared in the sky above the target. Our battalion fired about 75 of this special kind of shell over targets in and near Wiltz. A few fires were started, and some Germans must have received severe burns. It was the equal of any 4th of July or New Year's display of fireworks that I had seen.

On January 3, 1945, I was relieved without further adventures.

During this time, my letters consisted largely of thanks for food received and requests for more. I thought that the War Department reported wounds to the immediate family as it did deaths, and I therefore informed my parents that I had received a scratch on my head when my jeep hit a mine. There was no cause to worry. On January 7, my birthday, I added that the scab had just come off and that I had received the Purple Heart. Never had that medal been bestowed for the loss of fewer drops of blood.

My chief complaint was that the German offensive had delayed the mail. On January 19, 1945, I received a letter from home dated December 17, 1944. I wrote back: "They seem to lack transportation for mail, but they certainly don't for those fool cigarettes. Everyone has more than he knows what to do with."

The weather was also a frequent topic. For over a month, not a flake of snow melted even in the "heat" of the day. The temperature must have dropped to near zero on many nights. It wasn't too bad at the battery where a tent with a stove provided reasonable comfort. Infantry commanders began to assign a village as the day's objective. Soldiers did all in their power to take it, because it meant a house and hopefully a fire for the night. Once captured, it was virtually impossible to get them to move on to the next village until the following morning. The real challenge came when we had to spend the night in the open with, at best, one Army blanket. I don't see how we survived, but we did.

In spite of the suffering from the cold, I was impressed by Luxembourg's beauty. The evergreen trees were covered with snow, and when the snow on the ground became dirty, new snow fell to turn it white again. In the late 1980s, I spent several days in Yosemite National Park in early January. It snowed, but even the beauty of the white-covered evergreen trees and ground did not equal the scenes I still so vividly recall in Luxembourg.

There was a great demand for more Observation Posts and forward observers, but the severe weather made it mandatory to relieve them after a few days. Soon it became necessary to call on the sergeants who were chiefs of detail. I was glad to see that Currie was mentioned in the official account for firing on two tanks and dropping a shell in the midst of six Germans in late February. Early the following month, he knocked out two guns of an enemy battery. His excellent performance pleased me, as we had worked together at Fort Bragg and in Europe.

Our old friend, the 90th Infantry Division, was pulled out of the Saar Valley and moved north to help collapse The Bulge. On January 10, 1945, we were ordered to provide artillery support. The following day I went forward as an observer. I remember struggling up one hill after another through the snow only to descend each time into a ravine on the other side. On the 15th when I tottered down a steep hill, I reached Schimpach

Station, a settlement consisting of a station and a house on the other side of the tracks. As I remember, I had only Bradshaw with me. This meant that I was carrying half the radio weighing 46 pounds, plus my field glasses, maps, and other gear. I collapsed. Bradshaw offered to come back and help me. With offended pride I struggled to my feet and slowly hobbled across the track, too tired to be hurried by occasional sniper fire.

After giving my half of the radio to Bradshaw to establish communications, I stepped out on the tracks and began to search for a target. As I was peering through my field glasses, a bullet whistled down the tracks and removed the skin down to the bone on a portion of my left wrist. I jumped back, and the company commander called for aid men. Several came running and bandaged me up. This time a bandaid would not suffice, and I bear the scar to this day, but it was still not enough to get a day off. The company commander commented on my calm. It was a calm produced by fatigue, not courage. If the bullet had gone a tiny fraction of an inch to my right, it would have crushed my wrist. An inch to my left and it would have been in my head. It had been very audible when it whizzed by my ear.

We spent the night in the basement of the station. The next day we moved slowly forward toward Niederwampach, the division objective. It had just become dark when Charles MacClintock reached me. I remember lying in the trees on the side of a hill discussing whether he should relieve me then or the following morning. In the end, it was decided that he would take my place in spite of the problems of joining a company when it was digging in after dark. The next morning I learned that Charles had been mortally wounded by a mortar. He was a splendid officer whose ability was matched by his courage. He had been awarded a Bronze Star for his work during the fall, a richly deserved medal.

On January 23, I was again sent out as a forward observer. It was probably on this occasion that I became temporarily snow blind. I called for a round and couldn't see where it landed. Even when I could see, I rarely found a suitable target. We had no sunglasses to shut out the glare of the bright sun off the white snow. Since that time my eyes have been unusually susceptible to sunlight — my only long-range casualty from the war.

On the 25th I did fire on a machine gun with good effect, but the Germans came close to getting the best of it.

An 88mm shell hit 10 or 15 yards from me, and a fragment struck me between my right shoulder and chest. I could feel drops of blood trickling down. I tried to raise my arm, but could not. I knew I had the "million-dollar" wound. I was obviously in no danger of dying or suffering permanent injury, but a month's stay in a hospital where I would be warm and well-fed seemed assured. There might even be an opportunity to flirt a little with the nurses. When I was released, spring would not be far away, I mused.

Bradshaw was the only man I had with me. He came over and helped me take off layer after layer until finally we reached my undershirt and my wound. Only a few drops of blood were running down. By the time the fragment had penetrated all my clothes and had been deflected by my dog tags, which had become wrapped around the shoulder strap of my undershirt, its force was spent. I had another band-aid wound, and my right arm enjoyed a remarkable recovery — but not my pride. I could not look Bradshaw in the eye. Happily, I was recalled that same day.

I might add that Bradshaw scorned these minor wounds and refused to accept the Purple Heart when he received one. Three months after he was hit, he learned that five points towards a discharge were awarded for each medal. He had a sudden change of heart. As his band-aid wound had been recorded by the medics, he was able to claim his Purple Heart, as did three other officers and men.

When I reached battalion headquarters, I learned that one officer and five men were to go on three-day leaves in Paris. It was the first opportunity our battalion had had to send anyone, and the colonel had selected me as the officer. Three days in Paris were not the equivalent of the month in a hospital I had momentarily dreamed of, but at least they were a start. During the preceding 30 days, I had been slightly wounded three times and had had to press hard against a haystack to avoid being totally knocked out by a mortar. I felt in need of a change. I found my duffel bag in the truck that carried our surplus clothes and dug out my dress uniform of blouse, "pinks," light-colored dress trousers, and low shoes. A bribe sufficed to get some women to iron the former two. Since my poker losses kept me stripped of cash, I borrowed back a total of $130 that White, Cass, and Hawks had won from me during the preceding months. When all was ready, we were taken to the rendezvous where we were to join vacationers from other outfits, only to find that the trucks had departed 12 hours before. The authorities had forgotten to tell us of the change of schedule.

Around the last of January 1945, another opportunity occurred for leave in Paris. This time we arrived on time, loaded into a truck, and were driven through Bastogne and Sedan, to Reims, France, where we spent the night. I went to the officers club with several other lieutenants and drank champagne, as I thought you were supposed to do in France.

The next day we went on to Paris. I was given a room in a first-class hotel with another officer. Dinner was a meal of many courses served to the accompaniment of an orchestra. The ceiling of our room must have been 15 feet high, and there were beautiful drapes on the windows. I headed for the bathtub, only to discover that there was no hot water. Instead of lounging in the tub for half an hour while layer after layer of dirt peeled off, I could barely muster the courage for a quick rinse. I later learned that the enlisted men had a less swanky hotel but had hot water. I would have enthusiastically traded my accommodations for theirs.

That evening I had a date with an attractive French girl I had somehow met. The next morning I wandered across the street and consumed a bottle of champagne simply because I was in Paris.

The headquarters of General Rogers, Blair's father, was nearby. Earlier, I had written to ask permission to marry his daughter. He had said that he didn't know how to reply as it was the first time anyone had made such a request. In my family, it was assumed that this was a first step toward the altar. With three daughters, my father was an old hand at handling such affairs, especially as I suspect that several suitors had approached him before he was certain of the intended bride's consent. Blair later told me that her father's only comment was "Thank God it wasn't Bobby," but he had given me the go-ahead. He warmly received me when I was ushered into his office. I had dinner with him that night, and we were chauffeured around Paris in his sedan.

The General also introduced me to his aide, Lieutenant Edward M. Carmouche, and evidently told him to provide any needed help. Carmouche was a handsome, cultured, polished young man from New Orleans who spoke fluent French. Our medic, Captain Bick, had made me promise to have my wound in the wrist dressed before he let me go on leave. He had made no such condition when I had been sent on a forward observer mission a week before. Then his intervention would have been most welcome. It might have permitted me to loll around the battery in a tent rather than enjoy the comforts of a foxhole in the dead of winter. Still, a promise is a promise.

I asked Carmouche to take me to an aid station. The expedition was something of a farce. The medics were doubtless more than competent to treat venereal diseases and hangovers, but I doubt if they had ever seen a gunshot wound. In an awkward, grudging manner, they did their best. Carmouche also took me to a clothing store that handled uniforms. I had my Silver Star, Purple Heart, and European Theater ribbons installed on my blouse. Carmouche also took me to an early evening performance of the *Folies-Bergere*. The General kept about a half-dozen front row seats for "visiting firemen," and we wallowed in huge leather chairs that could have held two men my size. I topped off the evening with another date with the French girl.

The historical and cultural attractions of Paris did not entirely escape me. I joined a tour of the city and had my picture taken before the Arc de Triomphe with the others on the bus. When I wandered into the Louvre, I met a French officer. He seemed delighted to think that he might have found a cultured American. A few minutes' conversation disabused him of this hope, as I revealed my ignorance in one comment after another.

I don't believe that I had ever been on a subway, but I quickly mastered the Paris Metro by its marvelous maps. Somewhere I had heard of Vincennes, famous for its royal chateau, but I was denied admittance by the military after I arrived.

Another landmark loomed far larger in my mind. When I saw that there was a Metro stop at the Bastille, I set out to see that wonderful old fortress where so many notable persons in history and fiction had been incarcerated. Imagine my disappointment when I emerged from the underground and found a large empty square. Only now have I found the courage to recount this story. Almost as bad, I have absolutely no recollection of seeing the Notre Dame Cathedral, the Sainte Chapelle, and other wondrous sites on the Ile de Cité. The bus tour must have taken me there, but my French education had to wait until I returned for 18 months in 1952.

After three days and nights in Paris, we had to crawl back into our truck and be hauled to Reims where we spent the night. Once more, I dutifully drank much champagne although I never really liked the stuff. The following day we were left to our own devices. I visited the cathedral and drank more champagne. I noted one thing that irritated me. The quarter-master and other rear-echelon units in Reims were outfitted with rubbers to go over their shoes. Nobody in our battalion had a pair, and only a very few infantrymen were lucky enough to have the rubber shoes. While the frontline soldier wallowed in the mud and suffered from trench foot and frostbite, these so-called soldiers tiptoed around the paved streets of Reims without the slightest danger of getting their feet wet.

The following day we clambered on the truck and returned to the battalion after an absence of six nights and seven days. My first task was to ask my father who held my power of attorney to write checks on my account to settle my $130 debt to my fellow officers. I hope I had some left over, for how I could have spent that much in so short a time is beyond me. My hotel and meals had been free. I did send perfume to Blair and my mother and may have bought an Eisenhower jacket at this time. Most of my money had gone for champagne for which I was charged as much as $9 a bottle. I concluded my letter with "Really couldn't afford very many more trips, but this one was well worth it." In the end, my father picked up the tab, a real act of generosity at a time when a dollar bought ten times what it does today.

My trip also led my father to write to General Rogers thanking him for his kindness to me and praising Blair as "a very fine young lady." In response, the General declared:

> I couldn't have been prouder of his (Russell's) Silver Star ribbon, if I had won it myself — not to mention his Purple Heart with clasp! The Purple Heart is awarded for wounds, but I can assure you Russell shows no mark or other injurious effect from being wounded, and he still has his lovely disposition. He is anything but war weary, which is the term for describing those who are worn out.
>
> As I wrote Blair, she could not possibly have selected a boy that I was more pleased with.

Such sentiments were a far cry from Blair's memory of his comment that her choice could have been worse. I suspect that the General had resigned himself to the inevitable and was determined to make the best of a bad situation.

When I wrote my father, I took the opportunity to comment on my choice of a bride: "Blair is quite a catch. She is making a lot of her own clothes and can cook." Then in an allusion to my tentative decision to return to school on the G.I. Bill, I added: "Besides that she wants to support me while I go to school after the war. . . . Blair is making somewhere between $200 and $250 now which isn't chicken feed."

Actually she was earning more than I was as a first lieutenant. Indeed, even if the highest conceivable value was assigned to the foxholes and K rations the government provided me, my total compensation was still inferior to hers. My father generously offered to pay for my future education, but with many thanks I said that Blair and I preferred to go it alone.

My Parisian vacation had not been long, but in my absence there had been changes. We had been driving to the northeast before I had left and had reached the town of Trois Vierges in northern Luxembourg. While I was away, our troops had turned to the east, secured a bridgehead over the Our River, and once more faced the Siegfried Line. More important, the snow had finally begun to melt, and we were confronted by seas of mud. Still it raised our hopes. After the mud and a mixture of rain and occasional sleet, the spring must come.

I had hardly gotten back to the battalion before an attack was launched to break through the Siegfried Line. I was with the infantry on February 6 when Habscheid was taken in a predawn assault. I established an OP in a house on the eastern side of the town just a few yards from the "dragon teeth" that marked the beginning of the German defensive line. From this vantage point, I witnessed part of the 90th Infantry Division's drive through the formidable German defenses. Our After Action Report credited me with neutralizing a battery on February 9 and firing on an enemy gun "with good effect" the following day. I confess I cannot now remember either event.

On February 16, I went on a reconnaissance with Captain Kilbourn to select two OPs that could be used to support the 11th Armored Division. I occupied one of them for several days but accomplished nothing. By the 21st, I was once more with an infantry company of the 90th and participated in the attack on Lichtenborn and the action during the days that followed. I was relieved when we reached a hill overlooking Waxweiler and the Prum River. It was the last time I was to act as a forward observer for the 90th.

I recall four other episodes that probably occurred when I had worked with the 90th. In the first, I was in a village when one of our 240mm howitzer shells landed on a barn killing 10 or 12 of our soldiers. I had nothing to do with it but was blamed by some. Fortunately, the lieutenant who had pointed out the tanks at Mairy was there and stilled the troubled waters.

On another occasion, I was with a company that was directed to seize a village in a night attack. The next morning I could not make my map square with the terrain features around me. The company commander insisted that he had taken the correct village. I dared not fire a few rounds to determine our location, because the front lines were fluid. That night we set out to take the neighboring village. About halfway there we were pinned down by machine-gun fire. Isenhour thought that I had been hit and bravely crawled to rescue me. The company managed to beat a retreat without any casualties. When daylight came, we found that we had indeed taken the wrong village and were far from where we were supposed to be.

The third episode occurred when I was assigned to the 3rd Battalion of the 359th Infantry, whose commander actually accompanied his men in battle. His nickname was "Foxhole" Smith. One day we lounged in a shallow ravine with several of Smith's staff and another forward observer who was on his first mission. He was shaking violently from head to foot although nothing much was going on. Foxhole commented that he had a lot to get used to. I responded that I didn't think anyone ever did. I have often wondered what happened to the lieutenant. Foxhole was awarded the Distinguished Service Cross, but he was forced out of the war when his jeep hit a mine in the Battle of the Bulge.

Finally, I remember one occasion when my forward observer team was in a woods that was being pummeled by the German artillery. Each time a shell struck a tree, it exploded and fragments scattered on the ground below. We were in considerable danger. I took my men out of the woods and into a field in full view of the Germans. If we hugged the ground, we were in no danger unless the Germans got a direct hit, for the fragments created when a shell exploded would fly over us. By remaining several yards apart, they could only hope that a lucky shot would get only one of us. They had too little ammunition to waste firing on a target that was unlikely to get a single man. As I remember, they didn't even try. The woods where they believed there was an infantry company was a more lucrative target. I can honestly say that I have never dreamed about any of my wartime experiences, but to this day when I am walking in the woods, I sometimes hear shells crashing through the trees.

I have always regarded the 90th as my adopted division, for as a separate battalion we had none of our own. We had been with them in good times at Mairy and in hard times during the crossings of the Moselle and Saar rivers. Finally, it was with the 90th that we successfully assaulted the Siegfried Line. The war was won, but it would take a couple more months before the Germans would admit it. The 90th's officers also came to appreciate us. In the unit efficiency report of February 27, they declared: "This organization has been used with complete confidence in its capability to execute missions identical to those assigned to our organic medium battalion."

In short, the artillery officers of this proud division said that we were as good as they were. They could give us no higher compliment, for few good units admitted an equal. The principal credit for our success should go to Colonel Frink. I shall always remember him telling me that few of us could be leaders, but we all could be drivers. His knowledge and drive had made the battalion what it was.

Chapter 7

The War Ends

*T*HE WAR WAS DRAWING TO AN END. Little did I suspect that I had fired my last round. As if to prove that all was nearly over, the 4th Armored Division dashed 44 airline miles in two and a half days, and on March 8, 1945, reached the high ground overlooking the Rhine River just north of Koblenz, Germany. In their drive, they captured 5,000 prisoners and destroyed much equipment, all at a cost of only 29 of our men killed. The infantry followed as best it could, cleaning up the numerous pockets the 4th had left.

Our battalion was assigned to the VIII Corps and given the mission of supporting the 87th Infantry Division. The roads were packed with men and equipment, and we had to wait our turn in one bivouac after another. It was not until March 15 that I clambered up the steep stairs in a church steeple on the outskirts of Koblenz. I had a splendid view of the roof tops of the city, the towering Fort Ehrenbreitstein on the other side of the Rhine, and, above all, the 45-foot equestrian statute of Kaiser Wilhelm I that stood on the point where the Moselle and the Rhine rivers met. There were Germans in the city, but they were hidden by the buildings. I could find no targets. Another observer may have had the same problem. He solved it by firing on the statue of the Kaiser. Perhaps he was registering on it, a legitimate mission because the statue was surveyed on the map. Perhaps it was sheer vandalism. Whatever his motive, one of his first rounds toppled the statue, one of the few hits on an isolated target I saw during the war. The broken pieces of the Kaiser and his horse still lay in rubble when I visited the city eight years later.

Our battalion was on the north side of the Moselle. On March 24, we crossed to the south side. I was extremely happy to use a pontoon bridge this time rather than an assault boat. I was immediately sent to an OP overlooking the Rhine that had been surveyed in and connected by wire with another observer and the battalion. We were to witness the infantry crossing of the Rhine at Boppard the following night. If our troops ran into resistance, we were to measure the angle to where we saw the flash of the German guns. This would give their exact location, and our battalion would open fire.

March 25 was an unusually dark night. I still vividly remember standing on the steep hillside and watching the outlines of our infantry as they pushed off from the shore in their assault boats. They reached the other side of the river without a shot being fired. A little later I heard the blast of a few rounds of an automatic weapon. Then again, all was silent. The Rhine had been crossed without air support or artillery preparation. I had congratulated myself on being assigned the duty of watching this crossing rather than being an actual participant. As it turned out, it would have been fun to have been in the first wave. Instead, I crossed in an assault boat after daylight came and the landing area was fully secured. The engineers soon installed a bridge, and three days later our battalion crossed the river and went into position near Boppard beneath the steep cliffs of the Lorelei, where a legendary siren lured sailors to their doom.

It took several days for our troops to consolidate their position on the east side of the Rhine. Then we took off again. Except in one respect it was like our charge across France. This time we were often put in bivouacs for several days and then allowed to run and catch up. On April 3, we covered 100 miles — a record. This was far better than sitting for hours on the side of the road as we had so often done in France.

During the first half of April, we still had occasional missions. On April 7, our battery was headed toward a bivouac when a captain from another outfit told Cass to pull off the road for a fire mission. Lee Cass was the only officer present, but he went into position and fired seven missions on tanks, vehicles, and personnel that were attacking a town. An observer in a liaison plane conducted the fire. With the help of C Battery, the enemy attack was broken up. During the mission, Colonel Frink came along and wanted to know who authorized Cass's actions. He then reported to higher headquarters and was soon awarded a cluster for his Bronze Star "for meritorious achievement in connection with military operations against the enemy on 7 April 1945 in Germany." He never apologized to Cass for his initial criticism or gave him any recognition. Over a half-century later, all Cass could say was "Frink was no gentleman."

During this period, I spent some time on reconnaissance, but for the most part I had nothing to do except to hang around the battery. Quickly I became as bored as I had been in our dash across France and sought any form of amusement. One day when I was sitting beside a barn, I noticed a lot of pigeons flying in and out. I telephoned Captain Kilbourn, our intelligence officer, with the suggestion that they might be carrier pigeons the Germans were using to send military information. He took me seriously and contacted corps headquarters. Soon I received the query: were these male or female pigeons? Apparently corps believed only one sex was used as carriers. I thought a few minutes and then phoned back for information on how to tell a male pigeon from a female. This time I received no reply. Whether Kilbourn, one of our finest officers, realized that I was kidding and dropped the matter, or whether corps didn't know the answer, I have never learned.

With spring the weather improved. Leaves began to appear on the trees, and the grass turned green. Germany shook off the snow and mud of winter and appeared in all its glory — surely one of the most beautiful countries in the world. Its well-kept farms, tidy villages, and beautiful forests, its lakes and mountains can have few equals anywhere. German homes were more modern and better kept than any we had seen. In many respects we felt more at home than anywhere else we had been.

With blue skies and warm weather, my spirits soared. I recaptured some of the drive and love of adventure I had enjoyed when we first arrived in France, some 10 months ago. On March 28, I served as liaison with a combat team of the 87th Division. When we got out of radio range, our spotter plane relayed my messages to the battalion — a pattern we used in some of our April advances. I went along with our lead elements and reported back to headquarters where our troops were located.

Once in or near Thuringia, I unintentionally got ahead of our tanks. I remember arriving at a town of 5,000 or 10,000 situated on a hill. Happily, there were no German troops there and the civilian population ignored us. We sat on our jeep just outside the town and looked down at two small villages in a beautiful valley and waited for our troops. Soon our tanks appeared. We watched the careful way they maneuvered to insure that the villages and a forest on their right contained no traps. Finally, they reached the crest of the hill and found us sitting there.

"Well," I remarked to the major in command, "the tanks finally caught up with the artillery." He scowled and never said a word. I suppose we ought to have driven down the valley and told him that we had captured this town and that they could take the next one. But that would have made him just as angry, and we did get to see how the leading spear of an armored division operated.

Most of my activities were much more traditional. We were in a part of Thuringia that had catered to tourists and was full of summer homes of the wealthy. Around mid-April, we occupied a position by a small lake that served as a swimming pool and recreation center for a nearby town. I slept in a cottage and went boating. Some of our men wanted to fish. Having no tackle, they threw hand grenades into the water and picked out the stunned fish by hand.

Another time I was looking over an area where our battery might camp. The grass was several feet high, and I wandered a few hundred yards away from my men. Suddenly I came across two German soldiers. They immediately waved a white handkerchief. I signaled for them to get up, and the three of us began to walk through the high grass toward my men. Suddenly it occurred to me that I looked like the Germans' prisoner and my men might try to rescue me. Both were heavily armed with rifles while I was walking along empty handed. I had not intended to draw my pistol during the war, but I remembered that Stonewall Jackson had drawn his sword once in the Battle of Cedar Mountain, which had been fought largely on my great-grandfather's farm. I followed his example and pulled my pistol from its holster for the only time during the war. I then fell behind my prisoners so that there could be no mistake as to who was captor and who was captured. I have since learned that Jackson's sword was so rusted that he could not get it out of its scabbard, so he waved his sheathed sword with good effect. My pistol may have been in as bad condition, but happily I was not called upon to try to use it. After our battery arrived, five more Germans were found in the woods waiting for an opportunity to surrender.

We lived very comfortably at this time. There were many nice homes, often with indoor plumbing. Nearly all German houses had electricity, and there had been so little fighting in this area that the power was still on. The only problem was that the Germans had not evacuated the civilians as they had where heavy fighting had been anticipated. It was left to us to give a family its walking papers when we wanted their house.

I wrote my father:

> Have about decided I should deal in mortgages, because there is nothing I would rather do than throw helpless women and children out of their homes. The more they cry and complain, the better I like it.

Actually we were not as harsh as this sounds. There were always neighbors to take in the dispossessed. After our hardships, we deserved indoor plumbing, radios, and even a bed. I had let my men use furniture for firewood during the winter when it was dangerous to be outdoors, but with spring, we became more careful with our hosts' belongings. I did see an infantryman assigned to a foxhole improve his hard lot by bedding down on an oriental rug. He was not our responsibility; and after all he had been through, he deserved a little more comfort.

In the last three weeks of the war, the battalion assumed a defensive position near the Czechoslovakian border to the east of Plauen. Our orders were to wait there until the Russians arrived. I established an OP in a tower on top of a hill where there was a splendid view for miles around, but I saw no worthwhile targets. Our battery was nearby. When it became dark, I returned to stay in the house. There was so little to do these days that I wrote home for a book on bridge. To me it was a better game than poker. There were some players with my limited skill in other batteries, and with peace, we would be free to go back and forth.

The war in Europe ended on May 8, 1945. In the nine months and three days we had been on the continent, we had fired 51,000 rounds of ammunition and had lost only five men, two of whom had served with me. I was acting as a liaison officer when the news came. The headquarters of the unit to which I was assigned was situated in a beautiful home with paintings, statues, and flower gardens in full bloom. I almost regretted being ordered to go back to the battalion.

On my return trip, I purposely took a wrong turn and crossed the border into Czechoslovakia. I had looked at it for so long from an Observation Post that I thought I ought to pay a visit. There were several American soldiers in the small border town. We decided to press farther into the interior. After traveling about a half-hour, we suddenly realized that we had not seen a G.I. for some time. It was quite possible that the Germans had not heard that the war was to end that night. We decided to beat a hasty retreat. This time we accidentally took a wrong turn. Soon we ran into four Germans who surrendered. We put them on the motor of our jeep and took them back to our infantry. After that, we dutifully returned to the battery.

I passed a bottle of cognac around among my men and split a bottle of champagne with White and Cass. The radios in our house carried frequent news of the end of the war and much lovely music that even I enjoyed.

I wrote my mother:

> It was a beautiful day, warm and not a cloud in the sky. I had to go to an artillery demonstration. . . . It seemed strange to watch artillery shoot the day the war ended. . . . Suppose that is the Army. However, I enjoyed the trip to and from it very much. There are few parts of America that can compare in beauty with

Europe. Thousands of German soldiers were crowding the
roads as they swarmed in to surrender.

At all costs they were determined to become our prisoners rather than
the Russians':

> They came in trucks, on bicycles, in cars, and even brought
> their camp followers with them. Overhead the Luftwaffe was
> flying back to our airports to give themselves and their planes
> up. For the first time I fully realized the war was over.
> It really wasn't such a bad war, but one is enough. An offi-
> cer I met at the demonstration today accused me of gaining
> weight since leaving Sill where I had known him. Fear I shall
> have a hard time convincing anyone I am a war-weary veteran.
> Nevertheless am just as ready to go home as anyone else.

Then, in a postscript, I asked my mother to send Blair "a corsage of flow-
ers — either an orchid or gardenias on June 16." It was the day we were
supposed to have been married the year before.

As there were only three officers in the battery, I had many theoretical
duties such as acting as Mess or Motor officer. We had good sergeants in
charge of both, and I had never paid any attention to what they did. Indeed,
I was away from the battery over half the time. Imagine my horror when
I was instructed to join a team to inspect the vehicles of another battalion.
I didn't know how to turn the ignition on in anything but a jeep and a
truck. I said a prayer and signed the necessary papers after a perfunctory
inspection. I hope it was just another useless Army exercise.

On May 11, we withdrew 150 miles to an area in Thuringia just north
of Meiningen to assist in military government. The big problem was the
thousands of misplaced persons, most of whom had been imported to
work on the farms and in the small factories in the area. I was given a G.I.
who had been raised in a German-speaking family and assigned 20 villages and small towns in an area of about 100 square miles. Each morning
I set out in a jeep with my interpreter and Isenhour to visit the localities
in my jurisdiction. I would strut into a burgomaster's office and enjoy

watching him "jump up and bow and scrape. I was very stern," I reported with tongue in cheek, "and they tremble at my every word."

My mission was to find how many non-Germans there were of each nationality so we could arrange to send them home. To my surprise, some of the Russians who had been living with German farmers didn't want to leave. They had evidently been well treated, and with so many young German farmers killed or captured, there was a real need for them. I did not know at the time that many were Ukrainians and members of other subject nationalities who had as much cause to hate the Russians as the Germans had. The Poles all wanted to leave, and they delighted in tormenting their former captors. I described their plight in a letter home: "A sixty-year-old bearded German came up to me with tears in his eyes and said that a Pole had stolen his bicycle. It seems he was the village messenger," and could no longer perform his duties.

The one slave labor camp I saw reminded me of the frame barracks of our temporary Army quarters. It was even equipped with electricity and refrigerators. The principal differences were that their camps were surrounded by a fence. We were told that they were full of lice. When it came time to load the Russians into trucks, we found that about half of them were off looting. We had to take those we could find, so we piled them into trucks.

"Hope Joe Stalin straightens out the families when they get back to Russia," I piously reported to my mother. I could see how the British had messed up the Arcadians so badly, as Henry Wadsworth Longfellow described in his poem, "Evangeline." I suspect no effort was ever made to rejoin families once they reached their homeland. Nevertheless, from my perspective I could report home on May 17 that "Right now I am in the most interesting and busiest period of my life."

The chateau of the dukes of Saxe-Meiningen lay within my jurisdiction. It had been built in the 1830s and held little historical interest for me. It contained some art treasures and had been posted off limits before I got there; I decided not to disobey higher orders in spite of my temporary military occupation status, so did not visit the chateau.

I felt rather sorry for Lee Cass who had to remain at headquarters with the battery. I need not have. "He uncovered a naturalized American citizen. She wasn't pretty, but it wasn't fraternization."

I wrote home of one of our adventures. While we were drinking beer and looking out the window, we saw two Italian officers pushing a small sedan in which there were two pretty girls. . . . They had run out of gas and the Italians had pushed them to our Headquarters. One girl was French. She spoke five languages fluently. The other was Hungarian.

After a lively conversation in many languages, we "gave the girls some gas we had used to wash our clothes."

That night we visited an Italian military hospital in our district. The officers shared what little wine they had, and we listened to them sing. One officer explained to me that in Greece the Italian army was known as the "loathsome" army. I was surprised that he admitted it, until I finally realized that he was trying to say "love" army. They were doing all they could to disassociate themselves from their one-time German allies.

On May 16, we moved to another location near Bad Liebenstein where we were housed in a beautiful, modern 22-room house. There was a larger manor house nearby, but the baroness insisted that the Russians had stayed there and it was full of lice. The townspeople told us that she was lying to keep us from commandeering her home. They pointed out that she would not be staying there if there were really lice. I suspect they were right, but we were afraid to take any chances.

To occupy our new quarters, we had to dispossess a middle-aged woman and her daughter. Concerning the latter, I wrote on May 17:

> Am also carrying on an amour with an English-speaking German blonde who is the most beautiful girl I have seen since leaving the states. As we aren't supposed to fraternize I have to hide from the captain and a hundred men. Her mother is very strict. Another handicap is that we are living in her house, and she is sleeping on the floor in some nearby farmer's house. However German women thrive on mistreatment. In fact, we have a rendezvous in the potato cellar in my or rather her house. Sure is romantic. Can't wait to tell Blair.

Actually, the blonde's poor mother trailed her everywhere. There was no assignation. When I was driven to Nürnberg about a week later, Isenhour felt it safe to volunteer the information that Blondie had been flirting with the enlisted men as well. She was the most boy-crazy girl I have ever seen. In my better moments, I sympathized with her mother.

The move reduced my military government jurisdiction to four towns, but within this small compass there were two interesting structures. One was the manor house of the Baron von Butler. The new wing had been built around 1650, and the older part was standing when the first baron was created in 1415. When I entered the great hall, I saw a bearded old man who was reading to or teaching a young boy — a most picturesque scene. The musical instruments and other treasures of the Johann Bach Museum of Eisenach had been stored there to protect them from Allied air raids, which had destroyed many German cities but were unlikely to target an isolated manor house.

An old castle also fell within my jurisdiction. It had been bought by a Frenchman before the war. He had filled it with medieval antiques and Italian paintings. Most important, he had acquired a fine collection of Etruscan pottery 2,500 years old.

The need for an artillery battalion to assist in military government was obviously limited to the establishment of order and the repatriation of aliens, tasks that were completed in a few days. There was talk that thereafter we would go back into basic training. After defeating one of the finest armies in history, the very thought was as horrifying as it was ludicrous. I was therefore not altogether unhappy when I received orders from group headquarters dated May 20, 1945, assigning me to the Seine Base Section.

On the following day, I went by battalion headquarters to pick up my records and to say goodbye. I found that Colonel Frink had once again given me a superior efficiency rating. It was ironic that I, who had never been at home with firearms, should receive the highest possible efficiency rating while I was in combat, but only excellent ratings for the period I was at Fort Sill following my future career as a teacher. Frank McKeown, our warrant officer and assistant adjutant, told me that I had the second highest efficiency rating in the battalion. The number one spot went to Captain Bick, our medic. These overall standings that reflected our entire military careers were most unjust. There were many fine officers in the battalion who excelled in all aspects of the military art. I assume my "superiors" during my months in combat were due to the fact that I was the only member of the battalion to receive a Silver Star and three Purple Hearts. The first was a matter of being at the right place at the right time, and I am sure that many soldiers who received only one Purple Heart lost far more blood than I did with three. I doubt if Bick deserved to be number one, although he was certainly a caring and concerned doctor, and I am sure that I did not deserve to be number two.

I have often been critical of high-ranking officers, but my remarks should not be interpreted to include my superiors in the 949th Field Artillery Battalion. Colonel Frink always treated me with consideration, and I do not recall a single officer who ever criticized my actions as a forward observer. I was always my own most severe, indeed, my only vocal critic.

Of the battalion staff Captain Kilbourn was especially solicitous. He was in charge of the forward observers and was more aware of our problems and very likely our mistakes than anyone else. My battery commanders, Captains Seddon and White, were always supportive. Few junior officers could have been more fortunate.

While making my adieu at headquarters, the Colonel asked me if I knew what it was all about. I truthfully said no. I do wish that I had told him that the commanding general of the Seine Base Section was a friend of my parents. It would have prevented any misunderstanding, but somehow I could not conceive that General Rogers would assign me to his command. I would not want anyone with personal ties to be under me. I had never told anyone about Blair and our intention to marry. I have always kept personal matters to myself.

When I returned to the battery, I began to prepare for my departure. Each of us kept our rarely used belongings in a duffel bag stored in a truck. I dug out my blouse, pinks, and low shoes to wear to Paris. The duffel bag was still too heavy. I decided to discard the raincoat I had worn in Lorraine and at The Bulge. The lower right side had been blown off when my jeep hit the mine that had killed Speaker. There was a tear in the left wrist where the bullet had nicked me at Schimpach Station. Another hole marked the spot where a shell fragment had struck me between my right shoulder and chest. In the collar there were small cuts made by fine mortar fragments, while I pressed as close as possible to a haystack outside of Wiltz to avoid a direct hit. Such a raincoat would hardly do for a Paris assignment. I also abandoned the canteen with the shrapnel hole caused by a howitzer firing short in the Saar River beachhead. A leaky canteen was of no use and, of course, there was running water in Paris. Now, in my old age, I almost cry when I think of the wonderful mementos I discarded, and with them went some detailed maps I had preserved of areas where I had been in action. But at the time my only thought was that one phase of my life was over. It was time to close the book and start another.

The next day Isenhour and another soldier drove me to an airstrip near Nürnberg — a city truly in ruins. I made a point of shaking hands with Isenhour last. We had been through so much together that I wanted my last physical contact with the 949th Field Artillery Battalion to be with him.

I only wish that I had left a day or two later. On May 23, the group commander visited the 949th and awarded Bronze Stars to Isenhour and Jedrzjeck. I would have received one also had I been there. It finally caught up with me several months later. Apparently the recommendations growing out of the Saar River crossing had been resubmitted. I am glad that I was given a Bronze Star rather than a cluster to my Silver Star. I had undergone no greater risks than Isenhour and therefore deserved no higher medal. My only regret was that Speaker did not live to get the medal that he so richly deserved. I was unable to find a copy of Isenhour's citation in the battalion records and do not know what Jed was decorated for. He often served as my driver and was thoroughly dependable even under the most dangerous circumstances. It is likely that he was also involved in some other venture that I was unaware of.

I reached Paris on May 22 in the late afternoon. I was so sure that General Rogers had nothing to do with my assignment that I went through the same channels as any other reporting lieutenant rather than going directly to his office. I found to my surprise that no one was expecting me. I was given a room in a third-class hotel and directed to report back the next day. Again, I was shunted from one person to another until I finally reached a captain who grabbed me and took me directly to the General's office. Only then was the mystery unraveled.

It seems that General Patton had dropped by to see General Rogers shortly after the end of the war. They were old friends and shared a mutual love of horses. As the war had ended, Rogers would be free to attend his oldest daughter's wedding in Front Royal on June 2. In the course of his conversation with Patton, it occurred to him on the spur of the moment to ask if I could be assigned to him as his aide. Patton agreed. There had been no time to contact me. Indeed, the 949th had been in the First Army for about a month, and it had taken a while for the orders to reach the battalion. The General had about given up hope of finding me in time when I appeared on the scene.

General Rogers and his staff were quartered in the super deluxe Hotel Lotti. He offered to move me there, but I declined. I was not prepared for so much luxury and knew that I would not feel at home with all the brass. I suppose I should have accepted. It would have enabled me to become better acquainted with my prospective father-in-law and also to learn the duties of a general's aide that I was soon to perform briefly. I did have at least one meal with the General and his staff. Carmouche, his real aide, devoted considerable time getting me properly outfitted and showing me around. So many people were in Paris who had Front Royal ties that the General gave a dinner for us in his apartment in the Lotti.

General Rogers' staff included Lieutenant Colonel Walter S. Gabler, who had been a captain at the Remount Depot near Front Royal several years before. He had teamed up with another officer to rent a luxurious home just off the Champs-Elysées. He entertained a bunch of us there, took me to lunch at the Ritz, and found a balcony from which to watch a parade. Bim Cook, whose relatives I had visited on Cape Cod, was among his guests. I had last seen Bim at Fort Bragg in 1942, when he was in basic training. He had eventually gone to Officers Candidate School and had been commissioned a second lieutenant in the Air Corps administration and stationed in England. I knew that he had become a captain but was a little taken aback when I saw that he was now a major while I still sported my lieutenant's bars. What really threw me was to see that there were five bronze service stars on his European Theater ribbon to my four. And this was the first time he had crossed the English Channel! Evidently the Air Corps administrators shared the rapid promotion of the pilots and were entitled to wear each campaign star they earned.

On the afternoon of May 28, General Rogers and I caught the mail plane for New York. There were refueling stops in the Azores and Newfoundland, and we had to take a commercial flight from New York to Washington. The General left me in a car at the Pentagon building while he made his report. At my request, he had me assigned to the Field Artillery School at Fort Sill. I had fond memories of the place and thought it would be a wonderful spot for newlyweds should Blair and I marry. We reached Front Royal in the late afternoon of the 29th and were met by my parents and the Rogers family, including Blair who was there to attend her sister's wedding on Saturday.

I had dinner at Riverside and recounted many of my adventures while I ate. At around eight, I picked up Blair and we drove to the first pull-off on the way up the Skyline Drive. It was there we decided to get married. There was some talk of a double wedding, but there was no way we could get ready in three days. We hit on June 9, the following Saturday.

The Rogers-Geyer wedding took place at 8 p.m. on Saturday, June 2, with Blair serving as maid of honor and I as one of the ushers. As the guests departed after the reception, they were invited to return at the same time and place the following Saturday for our wedding. There was no time to print invitations.

We made one trip to Washington where I bought an engagement ring and a summer uniform. Blair and her sister switched dresses, but they had to be altered, and she also had to buy a trousseau. I tried to reserve the bridal suite in a Luray, Virginia, hotel, but it was taken. With an evening wedding and the scarcity of gas, the best I could do was to get a room at the second-rate George Washington Hotel in Winchester. My parents gave a big party for us on Friday night. Somehow we managed to get to the church at the appointed time the following evening. General Rogers had only his winter uniform with him, so I had to conform on that damp June day. He also wanted to wear his medals, and again I had to follow suit although I had only the Silver Star and Purple Heart. After the reception, Blair and I drove to Winchester, she in a pretty new outfit and I in my sweaty, wool uniform. The following morning my parents picked up their car and put us on the bus to Washington. We then caught the train to Princeton, New Jersey, where Blair had an apartment and her sister's car. On Monday, we drove to Atlantic City where we spent our honeymoon.

I wrote to Gene White of my adventures, and he responded with a wedding present. I thanked him, and this brought to an end my contact with the men of the 949th until the spring of 1997. My letter must have dumbfounded them, as they had no inkling that this would be my fate. I ought to have written Colonel Frink to tell him what had become of me and also to thank him for the consideration with which he had always treated me.

Even more, I regret that I did not send a letter to Isenhour telling him how much I appreciated his brave and able support in our adventures. No forward observer ever had a finer man to accompany him. I have never been much of a correspondent, and it has always been difficult for me to hand out praise even when it was richly deserved. My only explanation for my failure to write is that I was so confused by the rapid chain of events that a few months elapsed before I could digest what had happened to me.

With my departure from the 949th, the one exciting period of my life came to an end. That book was suddenly closed. With a wife and soon an entirely different career, a new book was opened. Until I began these memoirs, the door to this part of my past has remained closed.

Chapter 8

The Aftermath

LAIR HAD AGREED TO return to work at the Hayden
Chemical Corporation for a while so that other supervisors
in her laboratory could have a vacation. We bought her sister's Chevrolet coupe, and she set out for Princeton, New
Jersey. I proceeded to Fort Sill by plane and bus to begin
my new assignment and to find a place for us to live. I reported to the
school on June 27, 1945, where I was appointed instructor in Gunnery. My position and attitude were entirely different from what they
had been nearly three years before when I had taught in the Tactics
department. Then I was devoid of self-confidence and practical
experience. Now I had an abundance of the latter, and there was no
subject that I was more qualified to teach than Gunnery. I was also
familiar with the terrain and the procedures of the school.

I assumed that I would be quickly promoted. I had been in grade
for over two and one-half years and suspected that I was the ranking
lieutenant in the Army. During my previous tour at Sill, I had been
passed over because I had had one promotion but no field duty. No
such charge could be made now. I was devoid of military ambition

but had been embarrassed two years before when friends like Sonny Smith had asked why I had not been promoted. I wondered what they must be thinking now. My hopes were quickly squashed. Victory in Europe had reduced the need for officers, the school was cutting back, and promotions were frozen.

Two years before when I had taught in the New Division Officers Course, senior officers had tried to get me promoted. Now, I was not the one selected for a special effort. There was another lieutenant in the Gunnery department who had been commissioned and promoted to first lieutenant before I was. He had been awarded the Distinguished Service Cross and had been wounded while serving in a captain's job in Italy. Had he dug a little deeper in his foxhole and avoided a chance shot, he would have been a captain for a year or more. By doing his job like a good soldier, he had landed in a hospital and lost his chance at a promotion. He was a splendid officer in every sense of the word, and I had no complaint at my superiors' choice.

Socially, the Army post was now a disappointment. I missed Clyde Hooker, Thee Gilliam, and the constant flow of V.M.I. graduates through the school.

The one good thing was that I found a place to live much sooner than I anticipated. I heard that a fellow officer was being reassigned. Through him I met his landlady and managed to talk my way into renting her cottage on Washington Street in Lawton. It consisted of a living room, bedroom, dining area, kitchen, storage room, and garage all for about $50 a month. I wrote Blair enthusiastically about my acquisition, only to discover that her fellow supervisors had no intention of adjusting their vacation schedules for our convenience.

August came and then the Japanese surrender on August 15, 1945, before she escaped Princeton. Her mother wanted to go with her as far as Dallas to visit friends, and it took her ten days to get ready after Blair reached Front Royal. Finally, Blair arrived in Lawton sometime in September.

Oklahoma was still a "dry" state, but I had ordered a case of Old Granddad whisky through the officers club, which enlivened our stay. We had a few pleasant occasions at the club, and I showed Blair part of the military range including a dammed-up stream that made a splendid swimming hole and place to picnic.

My thoughts were on my escape from the military, however. I had accumulated 95 points, enough to insure an early departure, and on November 2, my duties at the school came to an end. I was in such a hurry to leave that I did not pick up the map case that had saved my life in the foxhole at the Saar bridgehead. I had loaned it to a fellow officer, and it would have delayed my departure an hour or so to get it back.

After visiting friends and relatives of the Rogers in Dallas and San Antonio, we struck out for home. Motels had scarcely been invented, and most Southern hotels were pretty poor. When we reached Roanoke, we splurged by staying in the beautiful hotel of that name. After a brief stop at Lexington to show Blair V.M.I., we drove home. With my accumulated leave and travel time, I drew pay until January 24, 1946, when I passed into the Reserves.

I was 99 percent sure that I wanted to be a history teacher, but I did consider the foreign service. I talked to a professor at Georgetown University about studying there and entering the State Department, but the idea had limited appeal. Another possibility was to seek a commission in the Regular Army. My father-in-law pushed me to apply. I knew that Blair loved the Army life and had difficulty imagining herself as the wife of a history teacher. It seemed wise to fill out the application forms. I would probably be turned down, which would settle the matter. If not, I could still reject the commission.

Meanwhile, I finally had been promoted to captain. The Army realized that some officers like myself with a good record on paper had been caught in situations where there were no vacancies at a higher rank and had spent many months, indeed years, in the same grade. In the 949th Field Artillery Battalion, no captain or officer of a higher rank had been killed or transferred during the war. There had been no openings. Perhaps the promotion made me more willing to apply, but it did not increase my love of the Army. I had ended up about where I belonged, but my promotion to first lieutenant had been undeserved and a source of embarrassment. My promotion to captain came at a time when it was meaningless. The Army was not the sort of career I wanted.

I was ordered to some place in Maryland to be interviewed and take examinations. I have always gotten A's or F's on interviews, whether academic or any other kind. I have never been observant enough to adjust to the circumstances. This time I blossomed. I enjoyed telling a bunch of colonels how to run the Army at the battery level. The exam was multiple-choice; in part, it tested general information, but there were a few questions designed to discover our attitude toward the military. In one question, the choice varied from saying that I always wanted to be in the Regular Army to seeking a commission only because there was nothing else to do. I honestly chose the latter. The physical exam was noteworthy only because I had my first and only contact with a psychiatrist.

I was neither surprised nor disappointed when I was not offered a commission. General Rogers checked and reported that I had done splendidly on the interview, satisfactorily on the exam, but the only letter of recommendation that was received had been less than enthusiastic. I had been asked to submit three names. As I remember, I listed Colonels Smith, Cox, and Frink. I had not contacted any of them to see if they would recommend me. Indeed, I had no idea of their addresses. The 949th had been deactivated in New Jersey on December 1, and I now realize that Colonel Frink had probably been released from active duty before that date. Colonel Smith was Regular Army and therefore the most likely officer to have been found. He knew nothing of my military activities since he had left the NDOC. I was a captain at the time I was interviewed, but my promotion may not have caught up with me at the time I applied. If Colonel Smith believed that I was still a lieutenant, I can see why he thought I had flopped. I made no attempt to find two other officers to recommend me, as I could have done. I had made my gesture and was more certain than ever that history and teaching should be my career.

It was one thing to decide on history and another thing to choose a graduate school. At my father's urging, I drove to the University of Virginia, at Charlottesville. It was then a beautiful but sleepy place. Their distinguished 20th-century historian had been a high official in the military government in Germany, and this was the period in which I intended to work.

Blair and I set off to visit the Ivy League schools. We spent the first night in her old haunts in Princeton, but I never talked to anyone about going to graduate school. The next day we went to Columbia, in New York City. It was a madhouse with hundreds of students milling around. The best I could do was to talk to a history graduate student who had something to do with admissions. He was most discouraging, and I believed that I could not be happy living in a large city. We drove on to Yale. Here I managed to talk to a professor, but New Haven, Connecticut, was a city and had no appeal. We had intended to go on to Harvard, but it too was in a metropolitan area. Blair was most uncomfortable with a pregnancy, so we turned around and headed back to Princeton. I was kindly received by Joe Strayer, the then relatively new chairman. I applied and was accepted. It was the wisest move in my life.

Because of changes brought about by the war, the spring semester did not begin until March 1, 1946. I got off to my usual slow start, but I eventually caught on. I took my general exams in October 1947, after three semesters of course work rather than the usual four or more.

During my course work I had fallen under the spell of Jinx Harbison and the era of the Renaissance and Reformation, and of Joe Strayer and constitutional history. I determined to combine the two and work on the constitutional history of the Renaissance. For my doctoral dissertation, I chose the meeting of the French Estates General of 1560.

Most of my fellow graduate students had served in the military during the war. From one of them I learned that Bob Goheen, an assistant professor of the classics and soon to be president of the university, was the commander of a Reserve unit in Military Intelligence. The Army wanted to form another unit at Princeton. I had been so indoctrinated in the concept of the citizen soldier that I thought it my duty to stay in the Reserves. On the other hand, I had also been struck by the number of the Reserve officers recalled to active duty, who were too out of touch with the military to perform their duties satisfactorily. I wanted to avoid such an embarrassment at all costs. As a European historian, my work as a civilian would keep me reasonably up to date. I applied for a transfer to Military Intelligence, and in October 1948, my request was approved. Unfortunately, the new Reserve unit had not been formed by the time I left Princeton.

During the winter and spring of 1949, I entered the job market. Strayer told me that I was to take no initiative. He would handle the initial negotiations. The G.I. Bill had brought a host of students into colleges, but it was generally believed that when the demands of the veterans had been satisfied, enrollments would return to the levels of the 1930s. As a result, there were plenty of one-year jobs but few indeed that offered any opportunity for permanence. One such position was at Emory University, in Atlanta, Georgia.

Emory had just received a substantial gift that enabled it to start doctoral programs in history and some other disciplines. There was no one to teach the period between the Middle Ages and the French Revolution. A specialist in my field was obviously needed. The problem was that the position called for an instructorship at $3,000. Instead of bringing me to the campus for an interview, the dean of faculty stopped by Princeton on a trip north to see me.

When an offer came through for $3,200, I asked Strayer what to do. He thumped the table and said that a Princeton Ph.D. was worth from $3,300 to $3,600. When I asked what would happen to me if they would go no higher, he said that he thought Princeton could take care of me for a year. I turned down the position, and Emory responded with an offer of $3,400. I accepted, and I have never ceased to be grateful that chance brought me to Atlanta.

I submitted my doctoral dissertation to Harbison on March 1, 1949, three years to the day after I had entered Princeton. A month or two later I defended it before Charles H. McIlwain, who had moved to Princeton after retiring from Harvard, Robert R. Palmer, and, of course, Harbison and Strayer. Three of them had been or were to become presidents of the American Historical Association. The fourth, Harbison, died before he could aspire to this honor, but a national prize for excellent teaching was named for him. It would be hard to imagine a more distinguished panel. After the defense, they suggested that I submit my dissertation to the Princeton University Press for publication. It was then that I caught the research bug. I decided to become an historian, not just a reader and teacher of history.

I had neither the time nor the interest to take an active part in the Reserves when I first moved to Atlanta, and there was no Reserve unit in the Military Intelligence, but in the fall of 1955 I learned that the Command and General Staff course was being offered. I could still squeeze into my uniform, so I bought some captain's bars and enrolled. I was so busy with my academic work that I did little more than attend classes during the first year and the two-week summer camps in August 1956 and 1957. I had had no contact with the Army for over a decade when the course began and was sick when I took the final examination. For some reason, I could not think and made a terrible mess of it just as I had my calculus exam at V.M.I. many years before.

By June 1959, I thought I had fulfilled my duty as a citizen soldier. I retired from the Reserves and thereby brought my military career to an end. The remainder of my professional life was directed toward purely academic matters; to the teaching and writing of history and to the numerous administrative chores that accompany being a college professor.

Suggested Reading

John Keegan, *The Second World War* (New York: Viking, 1989) is a good one-volume account of both the European and the Pacific wars. Norman Polmar and Thomas B. Allen, eds., *World War II: America at War 1941-1945* (New York: Random House, 1991) and I. C. B. Dear, ed., *The Oxford Companion to World War II* (Oxford: Oxford University Press, 1995) are excellent reference books. The multi-volume official history of the U.S. Army provides a detailed account of the various aspects of the war.

The most valuable volumes for the actions described in this book are Martin Blumenson, *Breakout and Pursuit* (Washington, D.C.: Center of Military History, U.S. Army, 1984); Hugh M. Cole, *The Lorraine Campaign* (Washington, D.C.: Historical Division, Department of the Army, 1950); and *The Ardennes: Battle of the Bulge* (Washington, D.C.: Office of the Chief of Military History, Department of the Army, 1965); and Charles B. MacDonald, *The Last Offensive* (Washington, D.C.: Office of the Chief of Military History, U.S. Army, 1984). The above volumes are based on the official records and some interviews with the participants. As the men involved were usually desirous of presenting their own and their units' actions in a favorable light, I have reported some of the less favorable rumors I heard at the time and suspect to be true. For General George S. Patton's life, see Martin Blumenson, *Patton: The Man Behind the Legend* (New York: Morrow, 1985), and for the growing recognition that Patton was our outstanding general, see Blumenson, *The Battle of the Generals* (New York: Morrow, 1993).

In *King of Battle* (Fort Monroe, VA: Office of the Command Historian, U.S. Army Training and Doctrine Command, 1992), Boyd L. Dastrup has traced the history of American artillery from its minor role in the early days until World War II and thereafter, when it caused most of the casualties inflicted by the American Army.

The war correspondent Ernie Pyle captured much of the spirit of the men in the ranks in the various branches of the service in *Brave Men* (New York: Henry Holt and Company, 1944). In a fascinating book, *Citizen Soldiers* (New York: Simon & Schuster, 1997), Stephen E. Ambrose has recounted the adventures of the junior officers and enlisted men, who actually fought the war. I had submitted my manuscript before Ambrose's book was published. Many things I expected to be criticized for, such as the assertion that the Germans were well-behaved in Normandy and fought as clean a war on the western front as we did, and the criticism of senior infantry officers for not leading their men in battle, may be found in his book. Equally repellent was the luxury in which the rear-echelon troops surrounded themselves, sometimes at the expense of the troops at the front.

I have found three books by members of forward observer teams. Edwin V. Westrate, *Forward Observer* (Philadelphia: the Blakiston Company, 1944) centers on the North African campaign in the winter of 1942-1943. Eugene Maurey's *Forward Observer* (Chicago: Midwest Books, 1994) is the account of a liaison officer of the 79th Infantry Division. K. P. Jones, *F.O. (Forward Observer)* (New York: Vantage Press, 1989) depicts the adventures of a scout corporal in a battalion of 105 howitzers in Patton's Third Army. None of the authors used the records of their units in the National Archives at College Park, Maryland, but each in his own way reveals something of the lives and actions of a forward observer team.

The XX Corps: Its History and Service in World War II, prepared and written by XX Corps personnel (Osaka, Japan, 1951) and the briefer *A*

History of the 90th Division in World War II (Baton Rouge, LA: Army & Navy Publishing Company, 1946) are profusely illustrated, deservedly laudatory accounts of their respective units to which the 949th Field Artillery Battalion was often attached. I did not discover John Colby, *War from the Ground Up: The 90th Division in WWII* (Austin, TX: Nortex Press, 1991) until long after I had submitted my manuscript. It is a detailed study in which the heroes and the cowards, the able and the incompetent, are specifically named and discussed. Bruce E. Egger and Lee MacMillan Otts, *G Company's War* (Tuscaloosa: University of Alabama Press, 1992) is the story of an infantry company in the 26th Division during the war. The 949th Field Artillery Battalion was attached to the 26th during the Battle of the Bulge, but I did not work with this company, although we were around Eschdorf, Luxembourg, at the same time.

Index

by Lori L. Daniel

150

Works by J. Russell Major

The Estates General of 1560 (Princeton, NJ: Princeton University Press, 1951; Johnson Reprints, 1970).

The Deputies to the Estates General of Renaissance France (Madison: University of Wisconsin Press, 1960). Studies presented to the International Commission for the History of Representative and Parliamentary Institutions, Vol. XXI, reprinted by Greenwood Press, 1974.

Representative Institutions in Renaissance France, 1421-1559 (Madison: University of Wisconsin Press, 1960). Studies presented to the International Commission for the History of Representative and Parliamentary Institutions, Vol. XXII, reprinted by Greenwood Press, 1983.

The Western World: Renaissance to the Present (Philadelphia, PA: Lippincott, 1966; 2nd ed., 1971). Printed as a two-volume work under the titles of *Civilization in the Western World: Renaissance to 1815* and *Civilization in the Western World: 1815 to Present*, and as part of a two- and a three-volume work in collaboration with G. P. Cuttino and Robert Scranton entitled *Civilization in the Western World*.

152

The Age of the Renaissance and Reformation (Philadelphia, PA: Lippincott, 1970), drawn largely from above work.

Bellièvre, Sully, and the Assembly of Notables of 1596, published in *Transactions of the American Philosophical Society*, LXIV (1974).

Representative Government in Early Modern France (New Haven, CT: Yale University Press, 1980). Studies presented to the International Commission for the History of Representative and Parliamentary Institutions, Vol. LXIII.

The Monarchy, the Estates, and the Aristocracy in Renaissance France (London: Variorum Press, 1988).

From Renaissance Monarchy to Absolute Monarchy: French Kings, Nobles and Estates (Baltimore, MD: The Johns Hopkins University Press, 1994).

A Major Family of Virginia (Fernandina, FL: Wolfe Publishing, 1998).